6 page preview

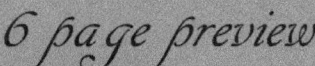

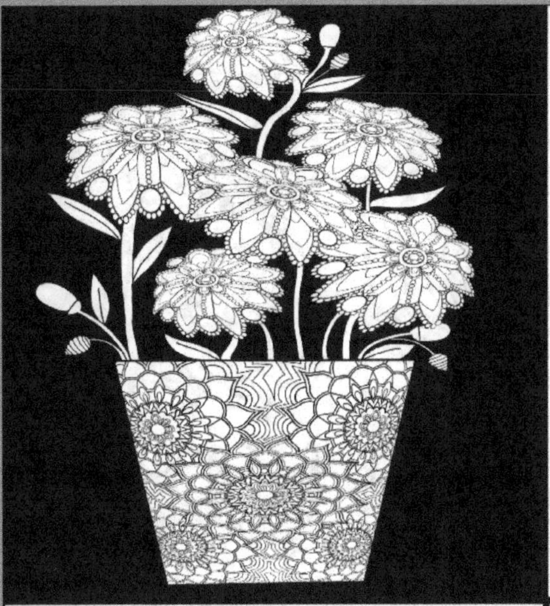

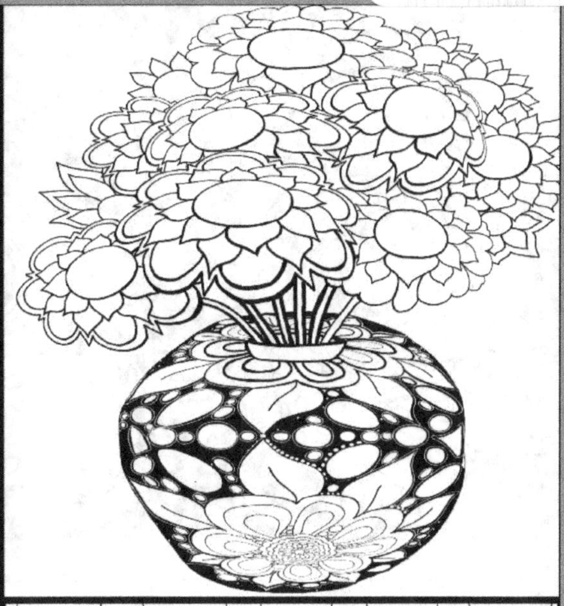

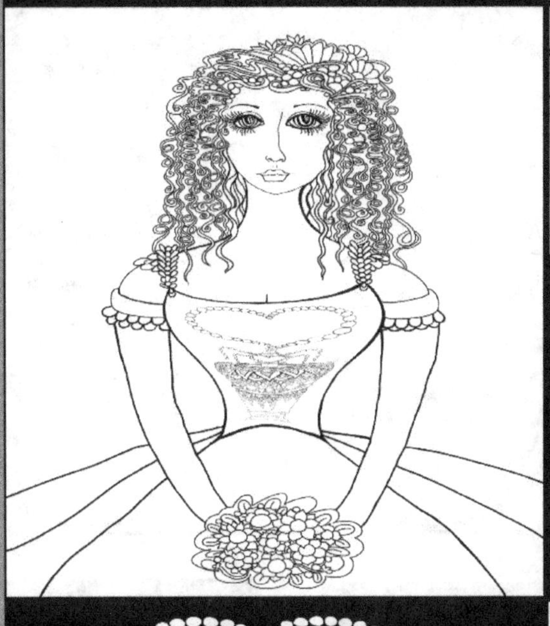

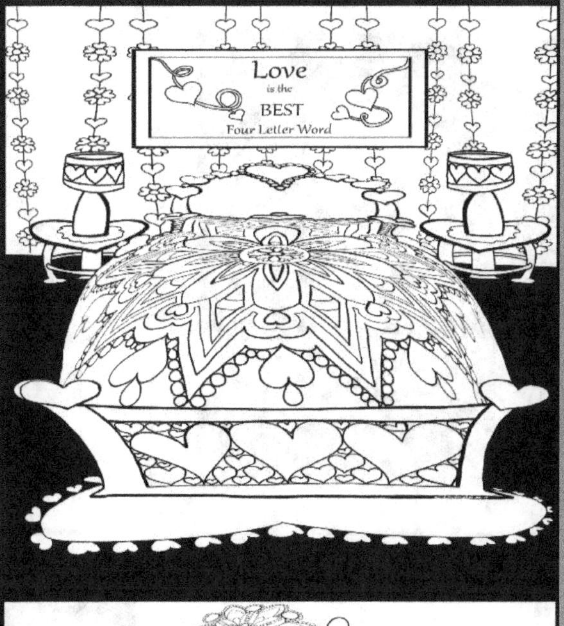

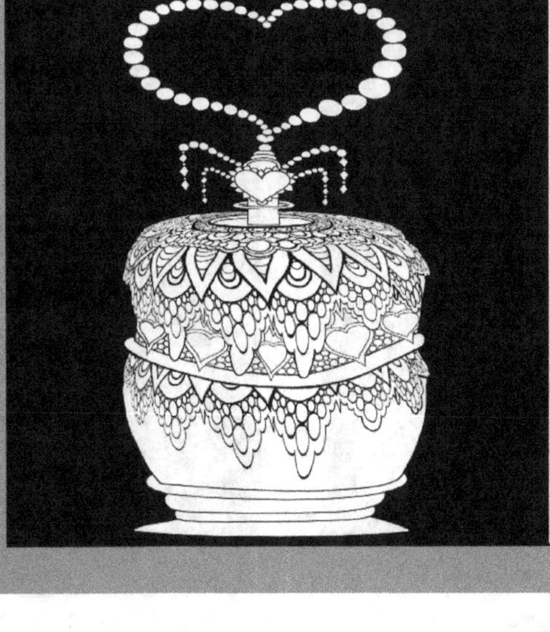

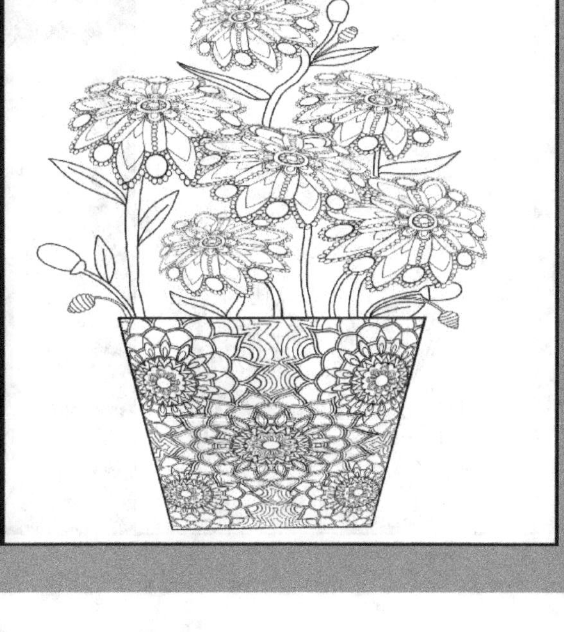

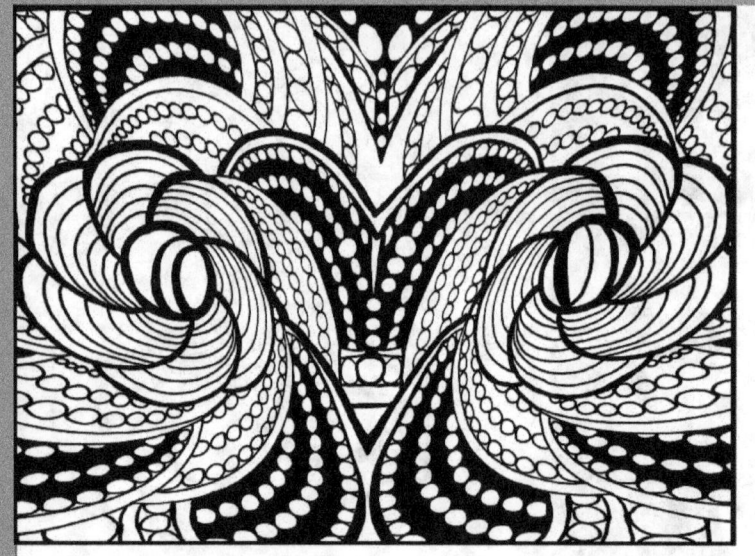
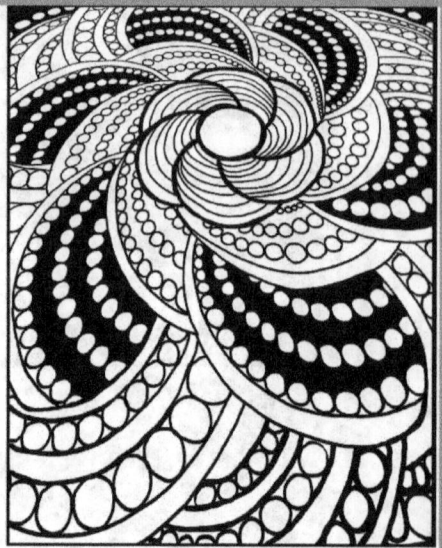
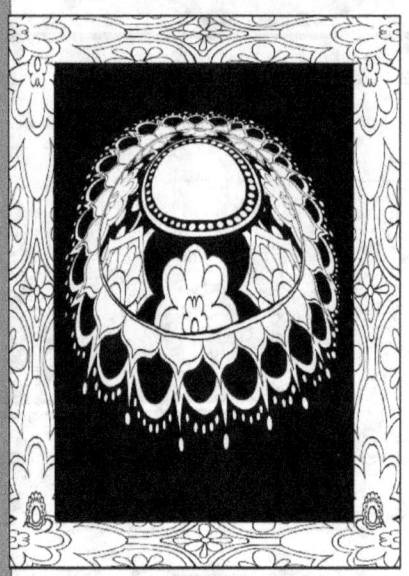
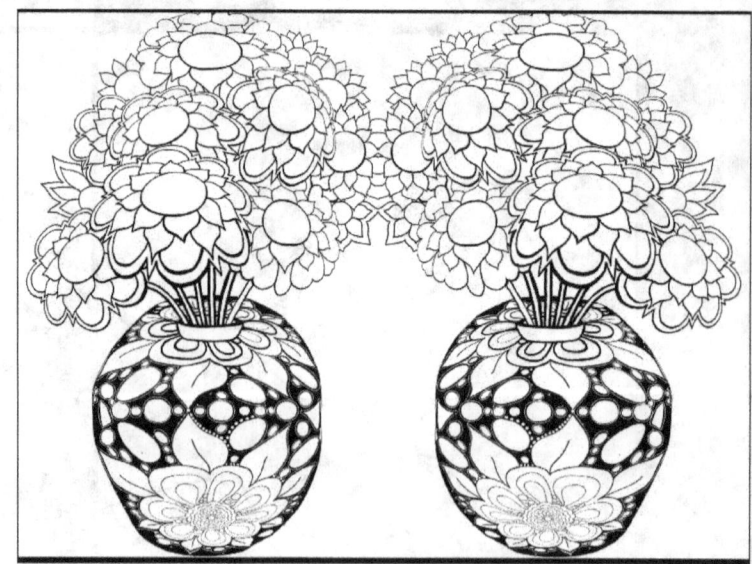
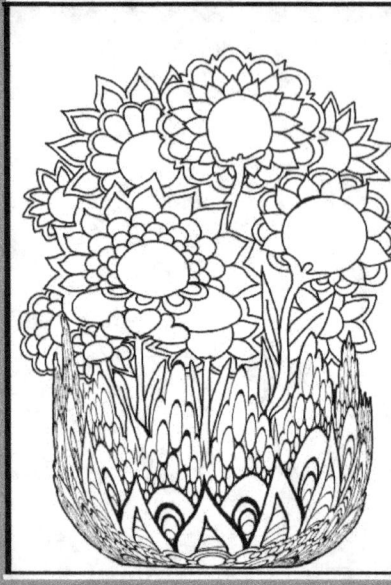
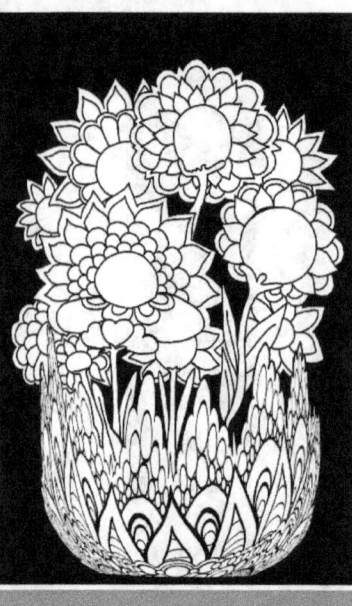
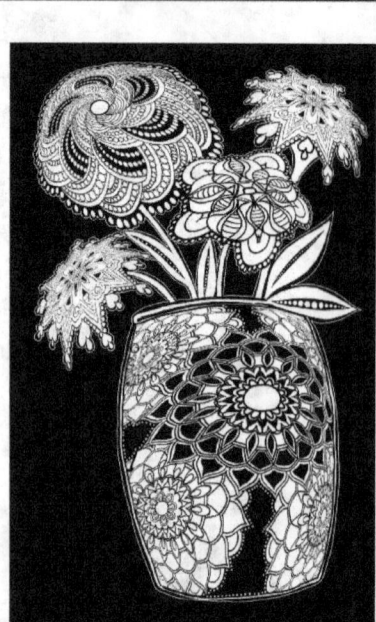

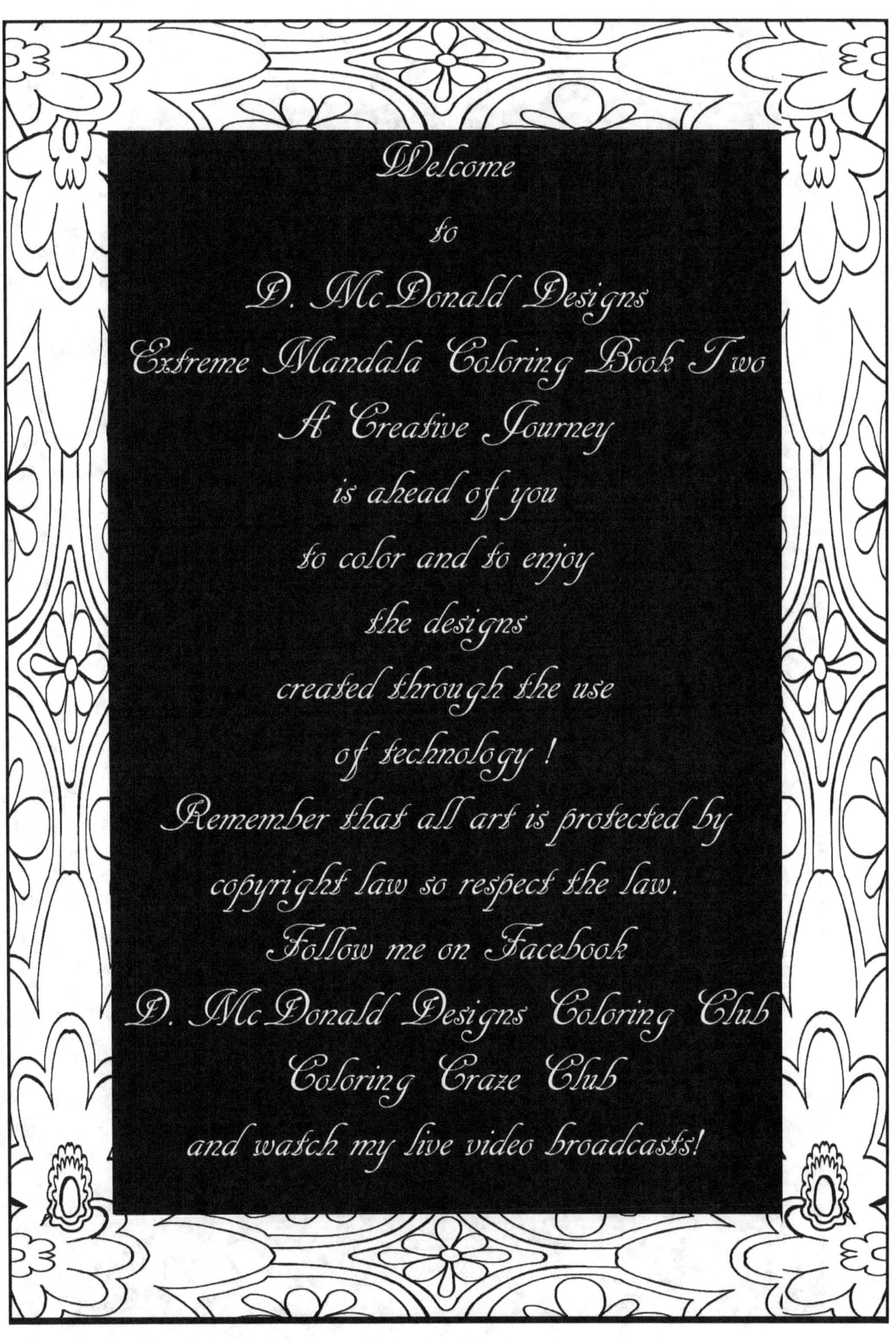

Welcome

to

D. McDonald Designs
Extreme Mandala Coloring Book Two
A Creative Journey
is ahead of you
to color and to enjoy
the designs
created through the use
of technology !
Remember that all art is protected by
copyright law so respect the law.
Follow me on Facebook
D. McDonald Designs Coloring Club
Coloring Craze Club
and watch my live video broadcasts!

Meet the Featured Cover Artist
Donna Pecoraro

As a lifetime New York City resident, Donna Pecoraro is part of a vibrant world of cultural diversity and is influenced in her work by the sights that surround her daily. She graduated from Queens College of the City of New York in 1979 with a degree in Fine Arts, but worked in the medical field and co-authored papers for medical journals. She is the single mom of a now 17 year old daughter and aspiring artist. After discovering Adult Coloring more than a year ago, Donna delved into the hobby, enjoying every aspect of it. She has collaborated with independently published artists and her coloring appears on several front and back covers of their books. Donna believes that the artists provide colorists with the base to create in a way that was never before possible, and that so many people have untapped artistic talent. Coloring is a way to enter that world and experience the thrill of creativity. Donna stresses that there is no limit to what you can do, learn, and experiment with in coloring, and that when you get into that flow, the benefits will amaze you!

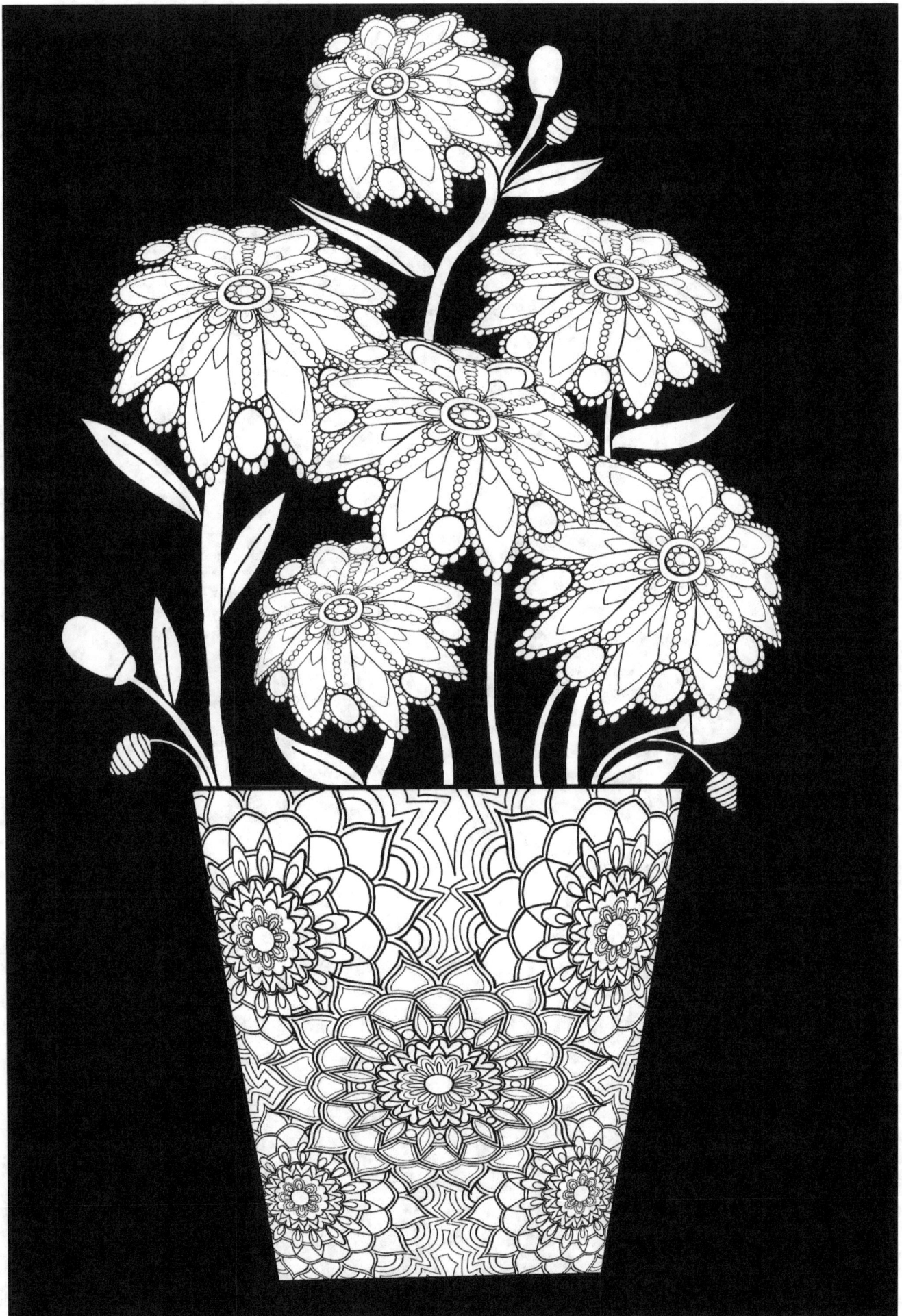

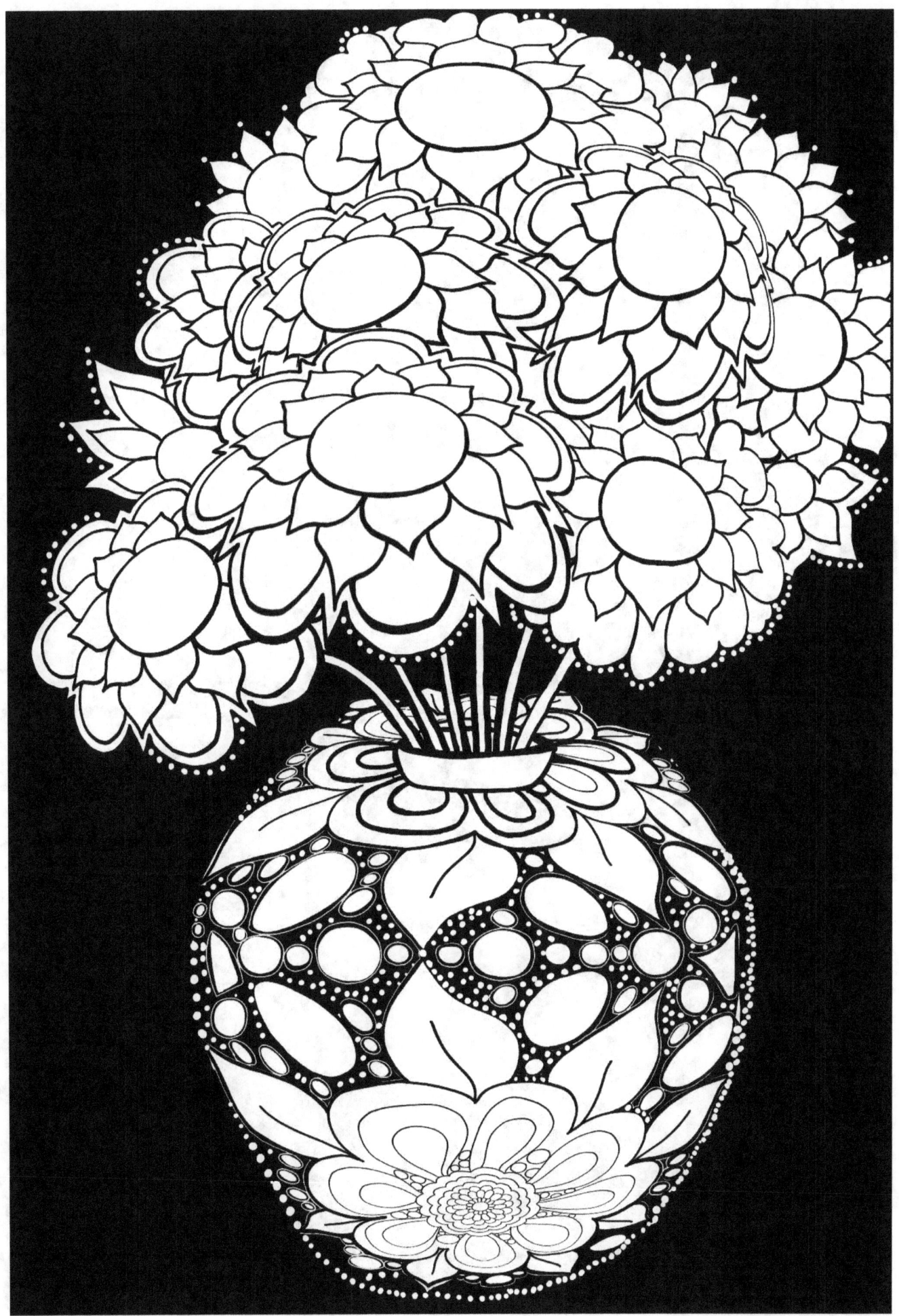

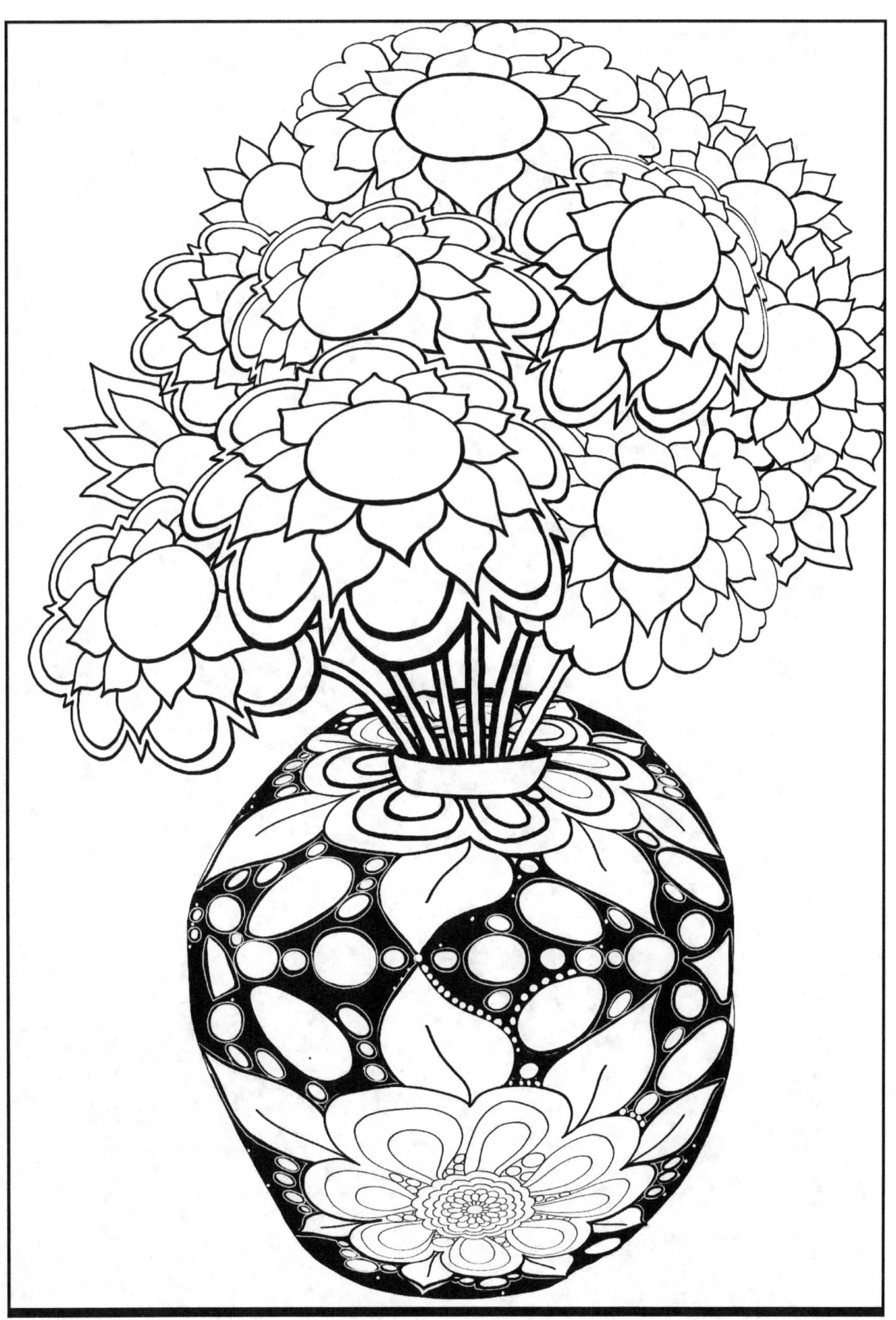

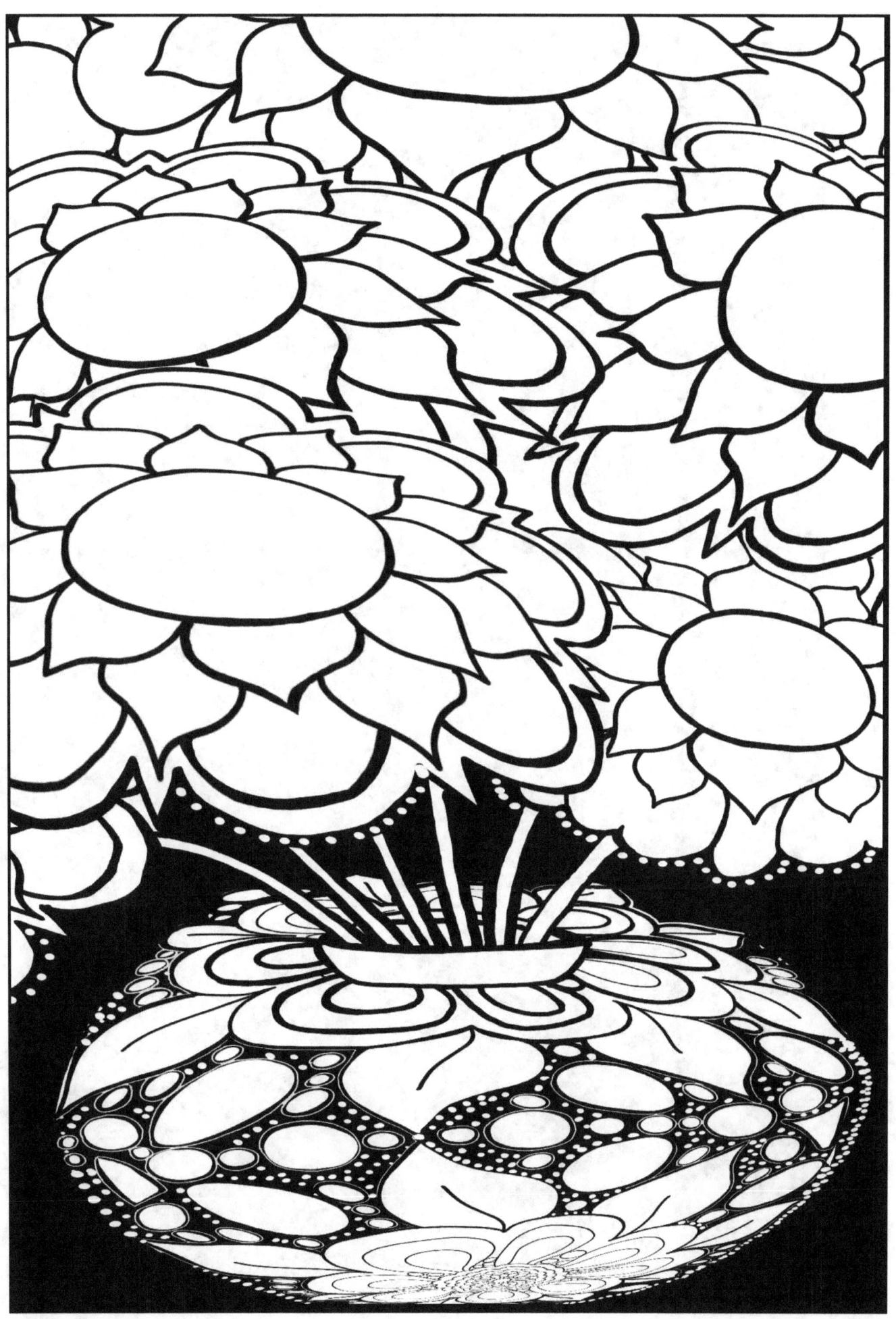

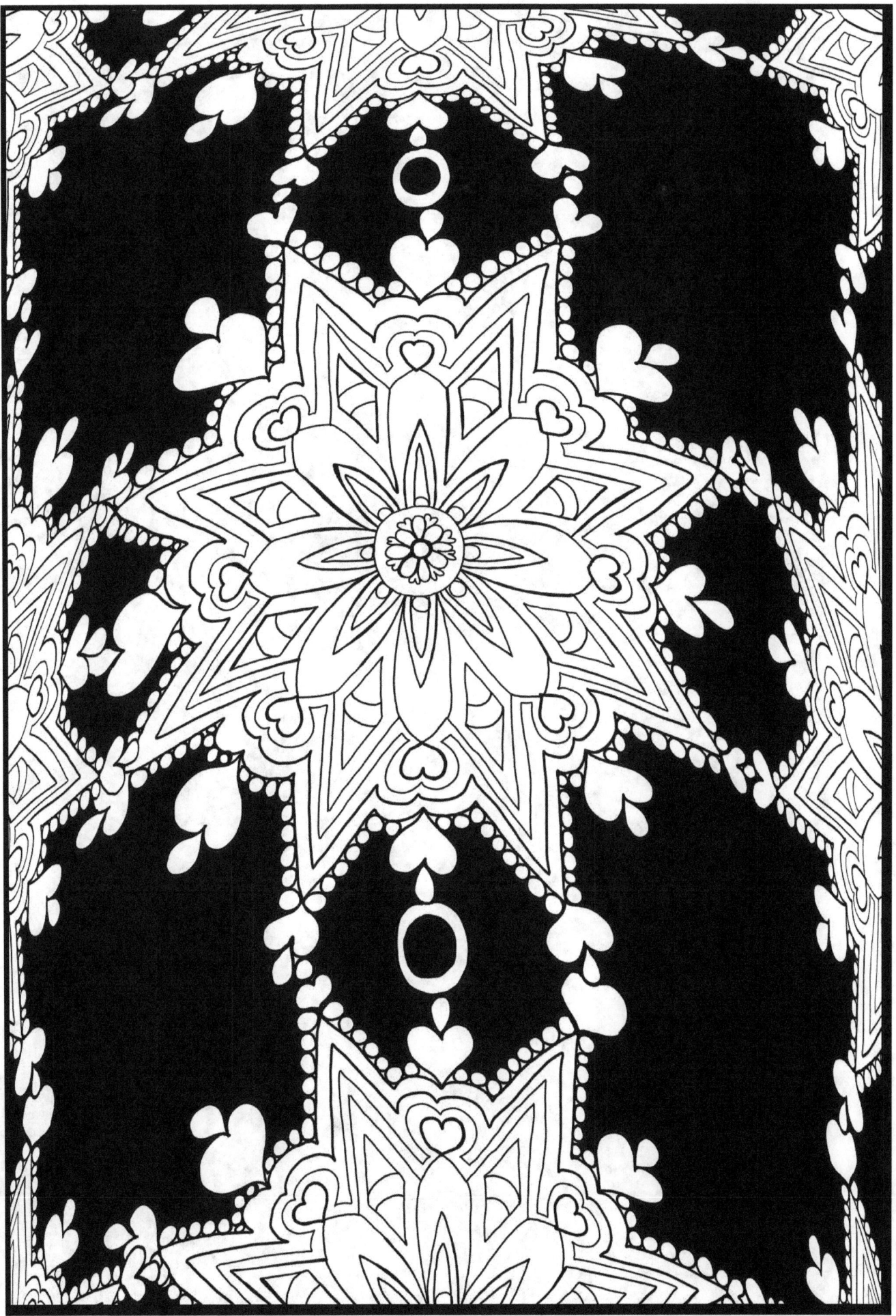

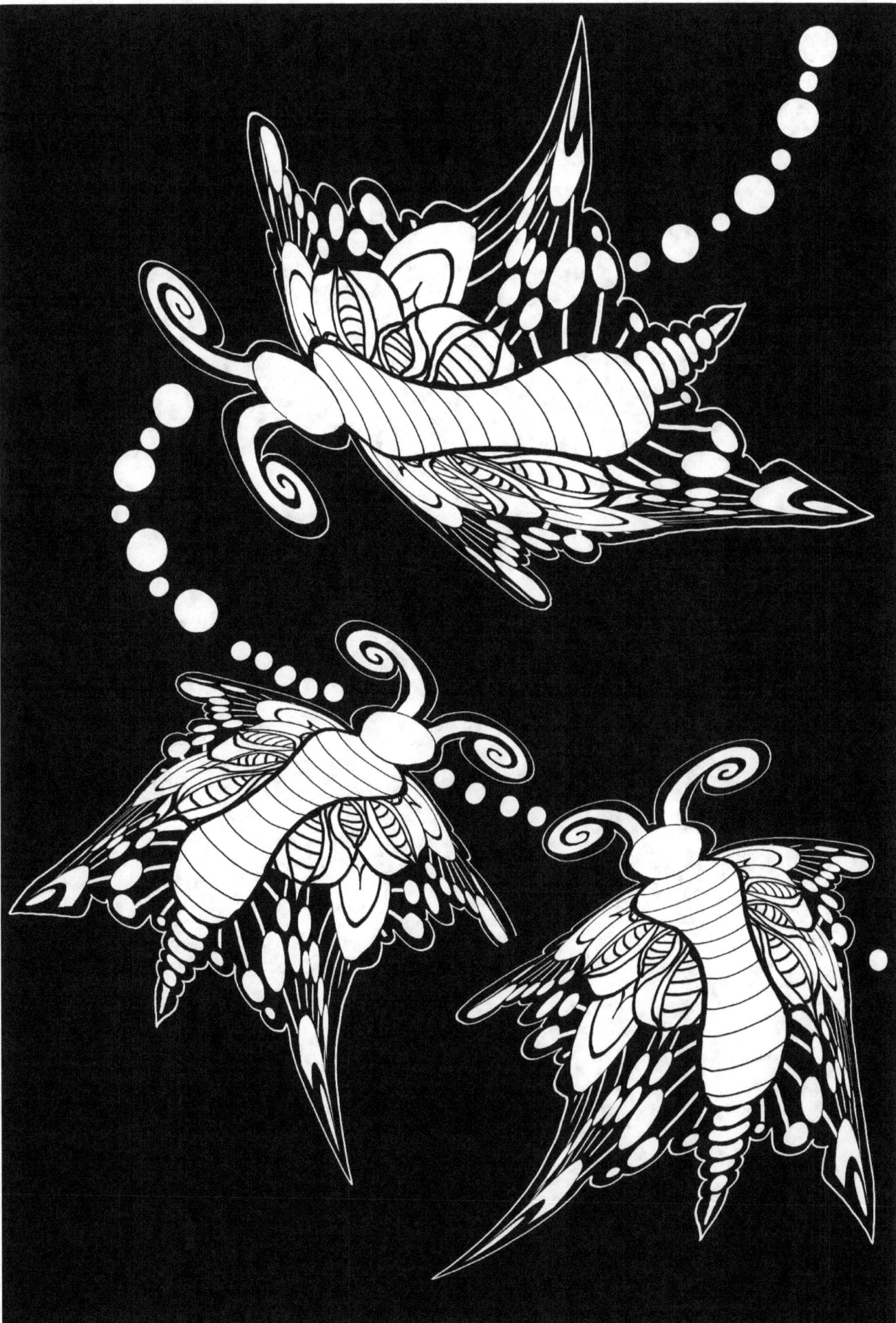

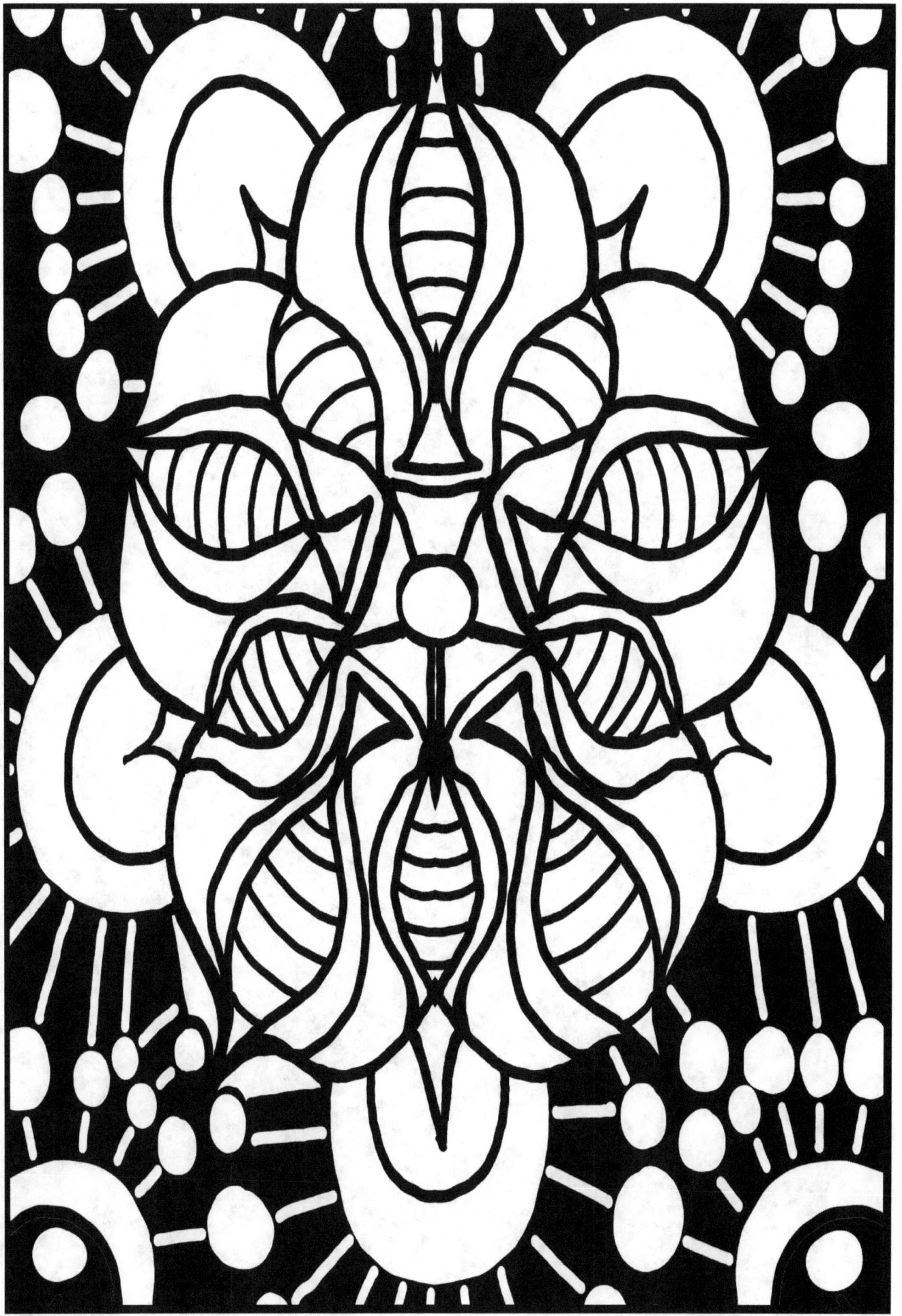

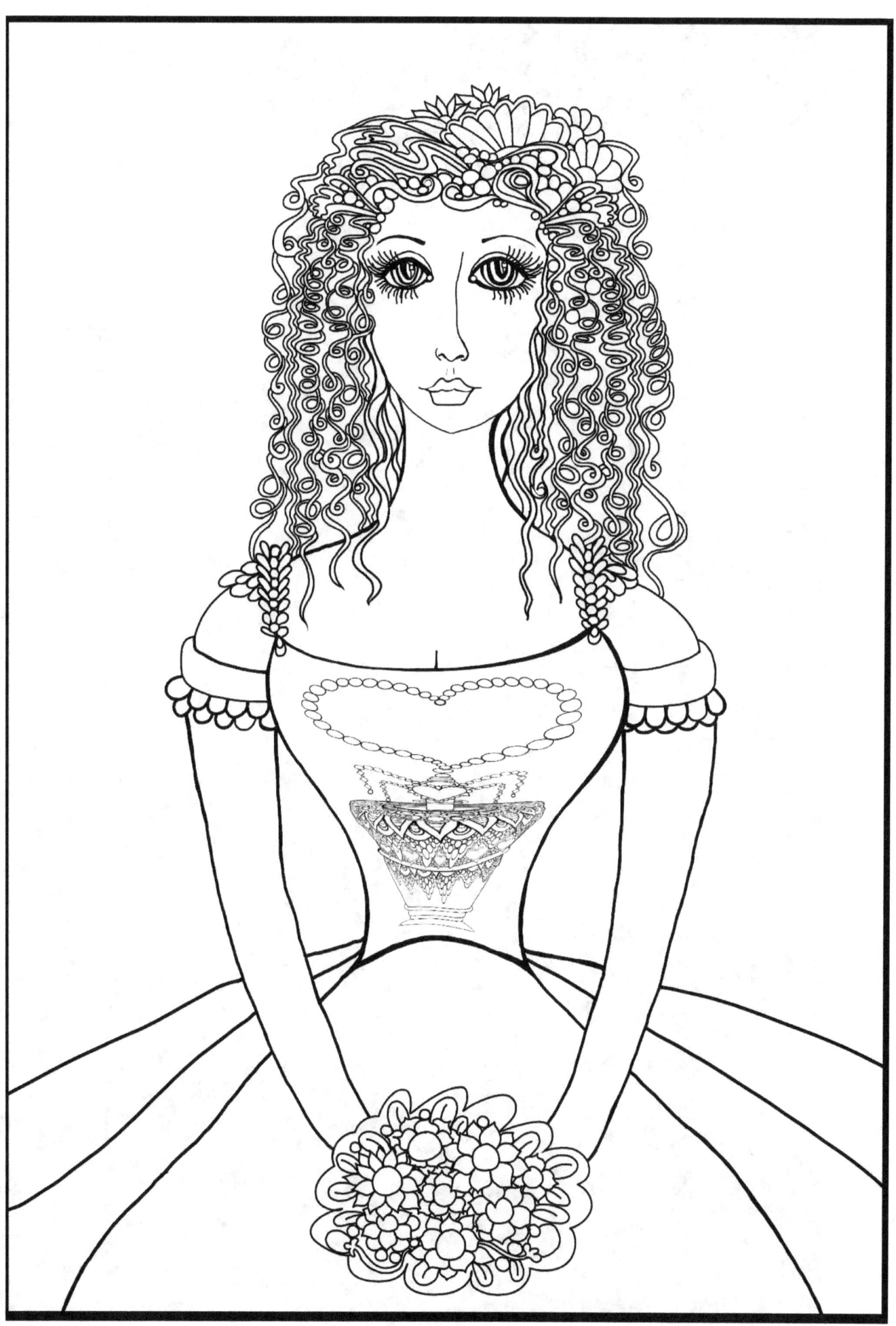

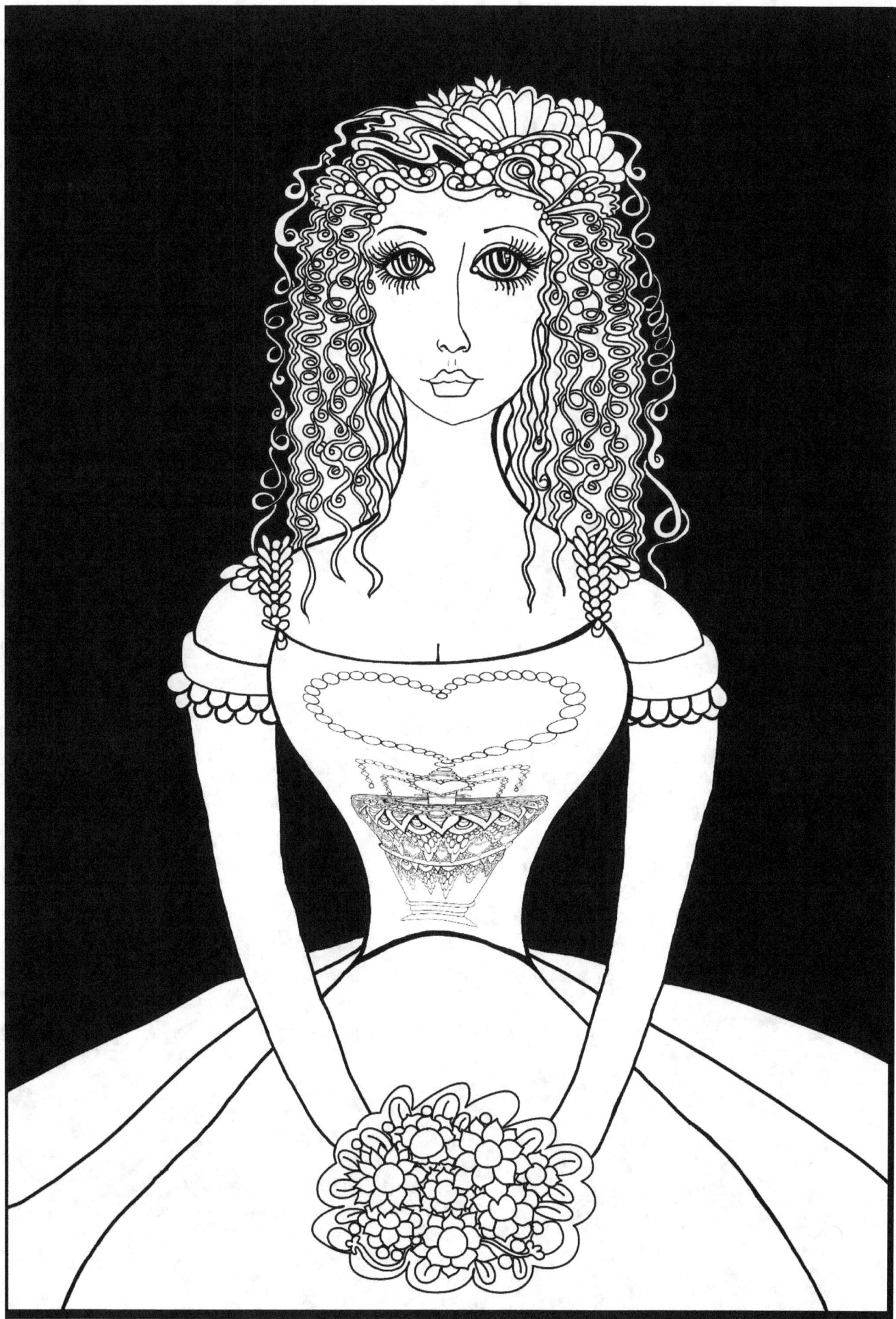

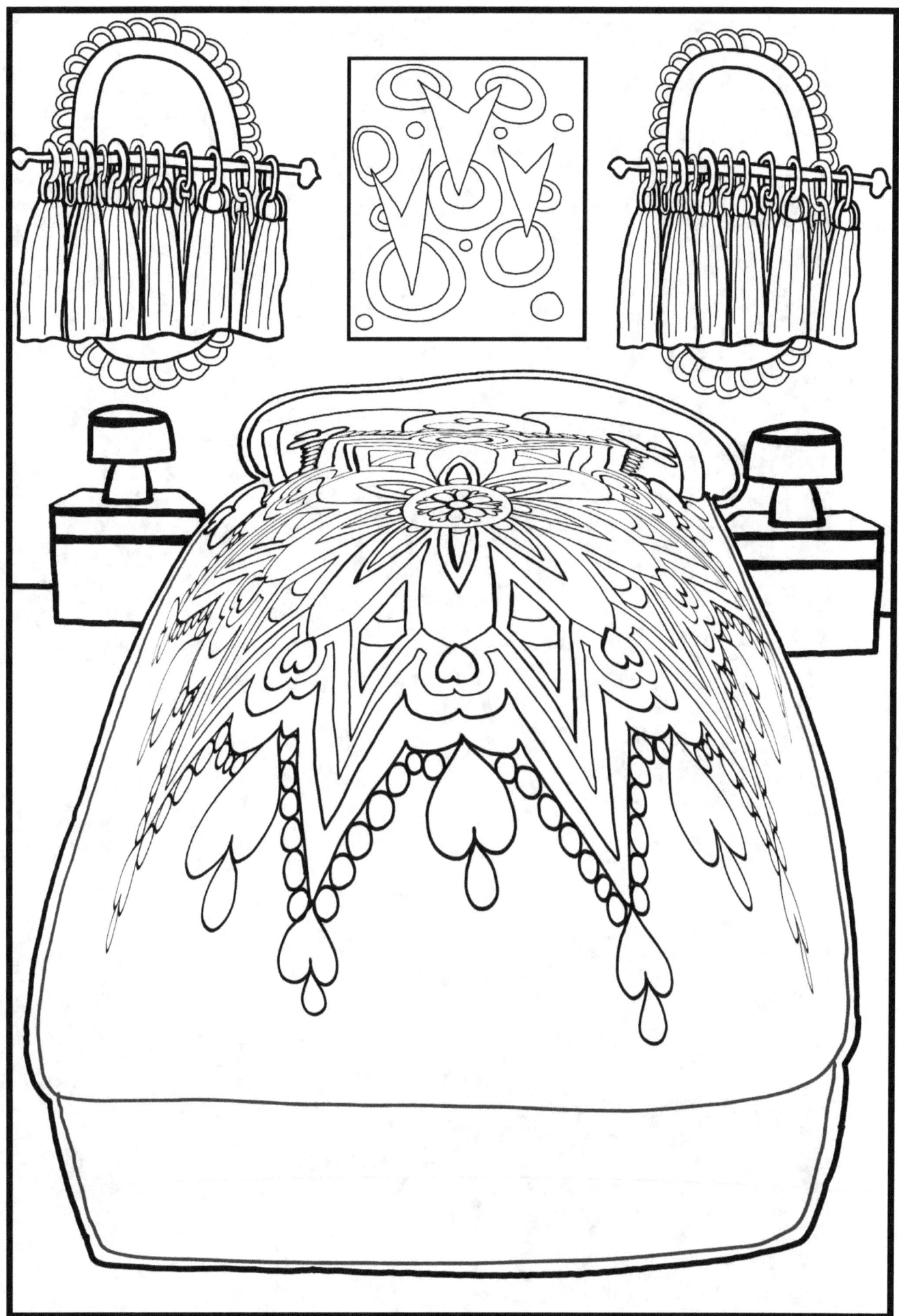

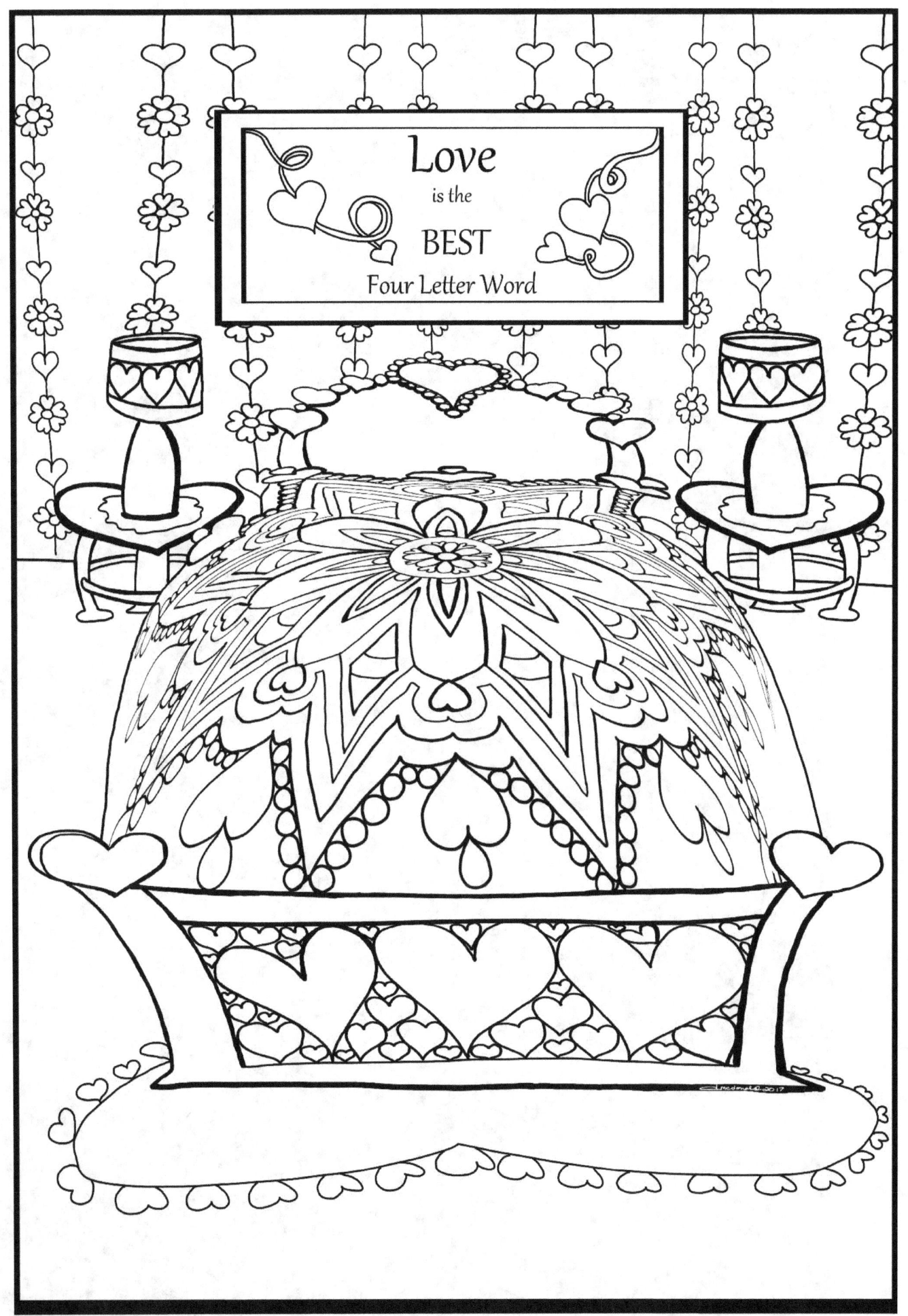

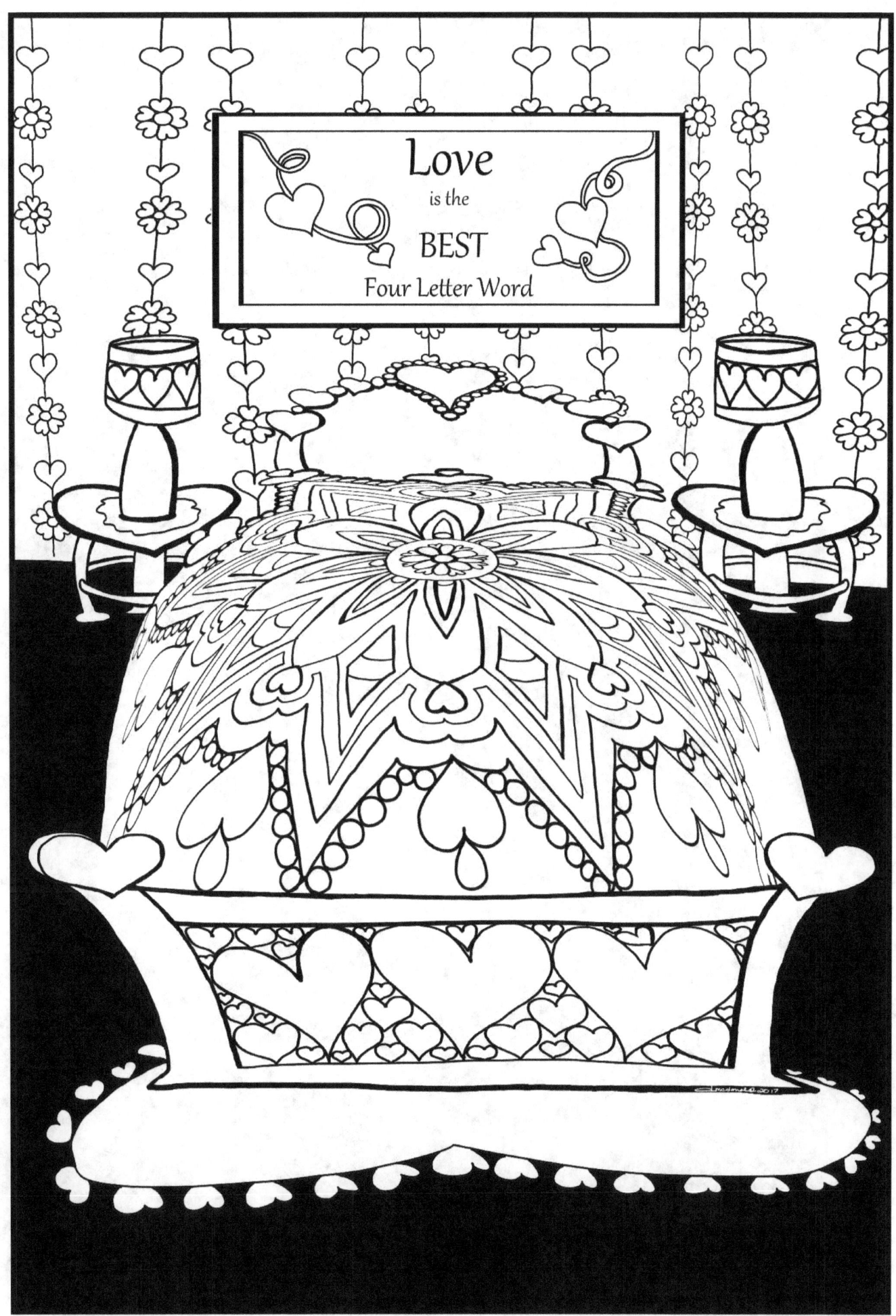

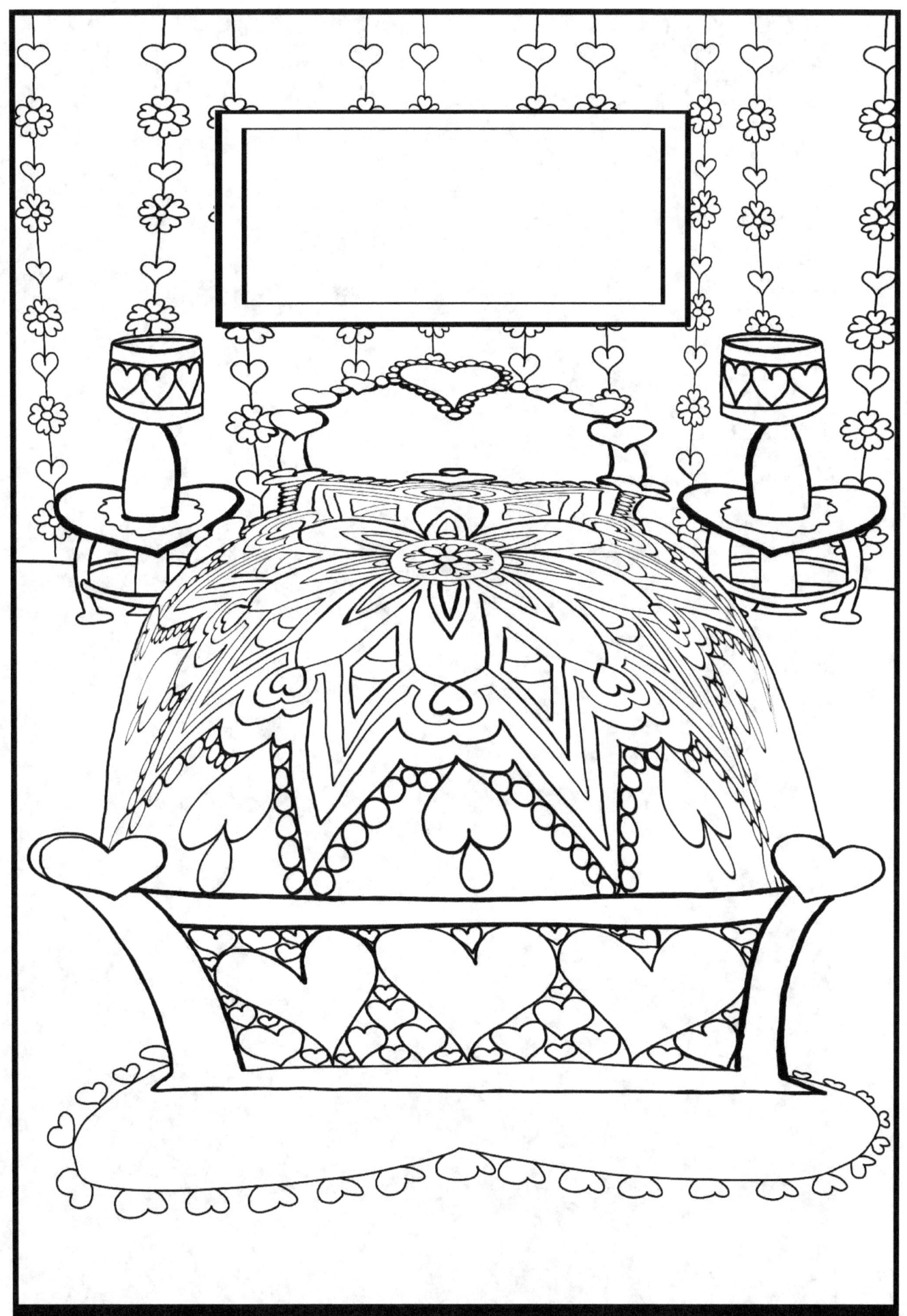

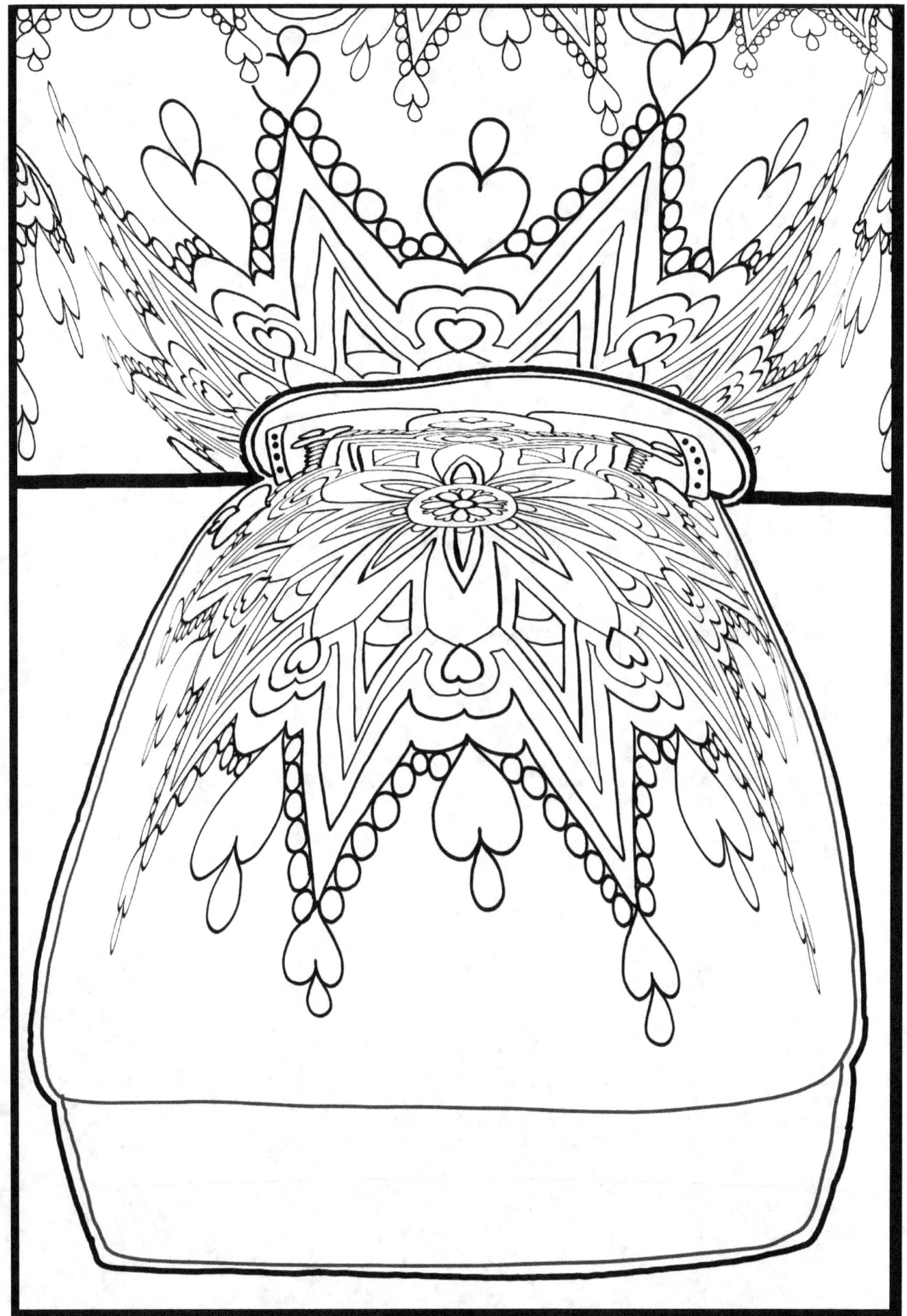

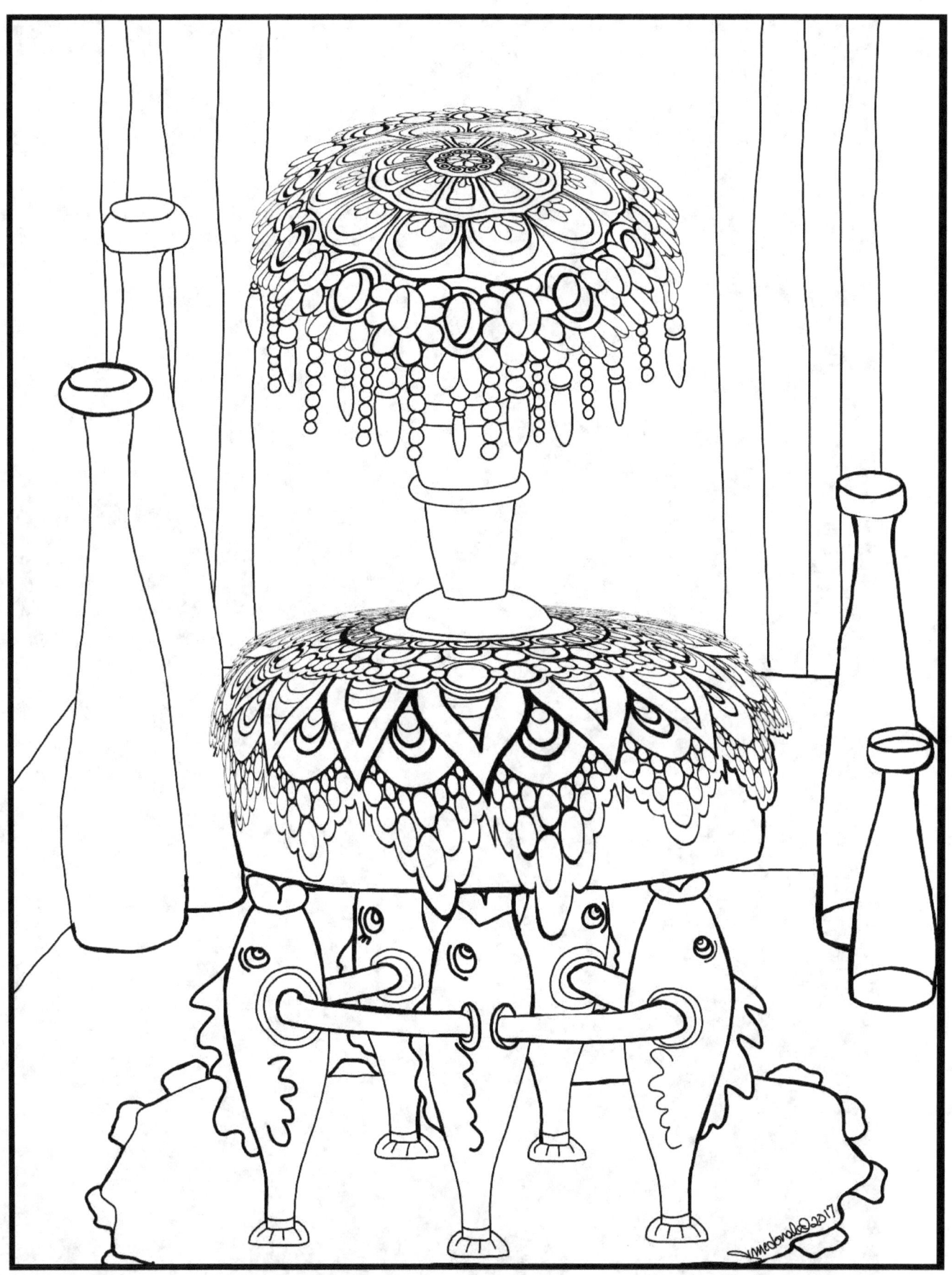

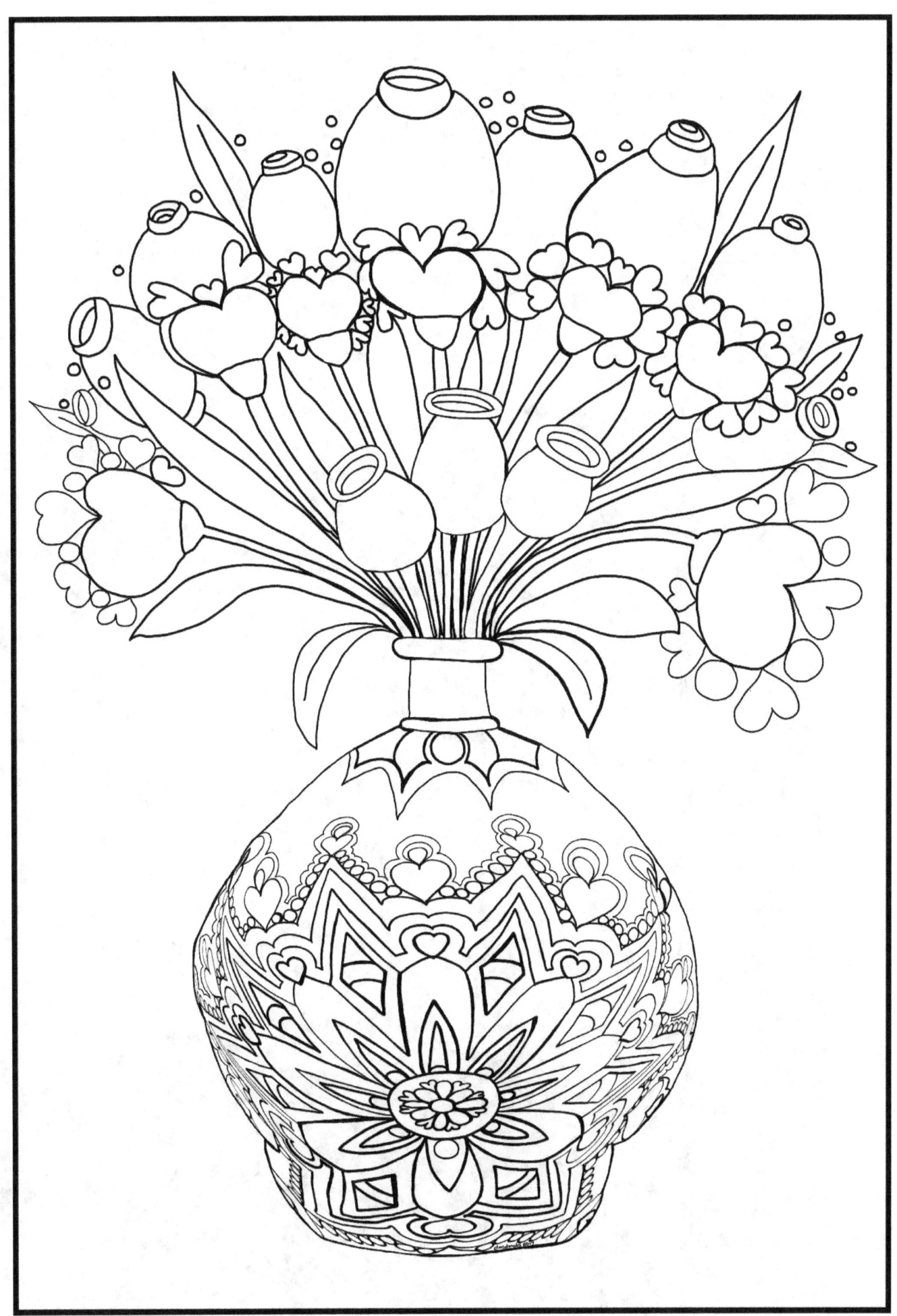

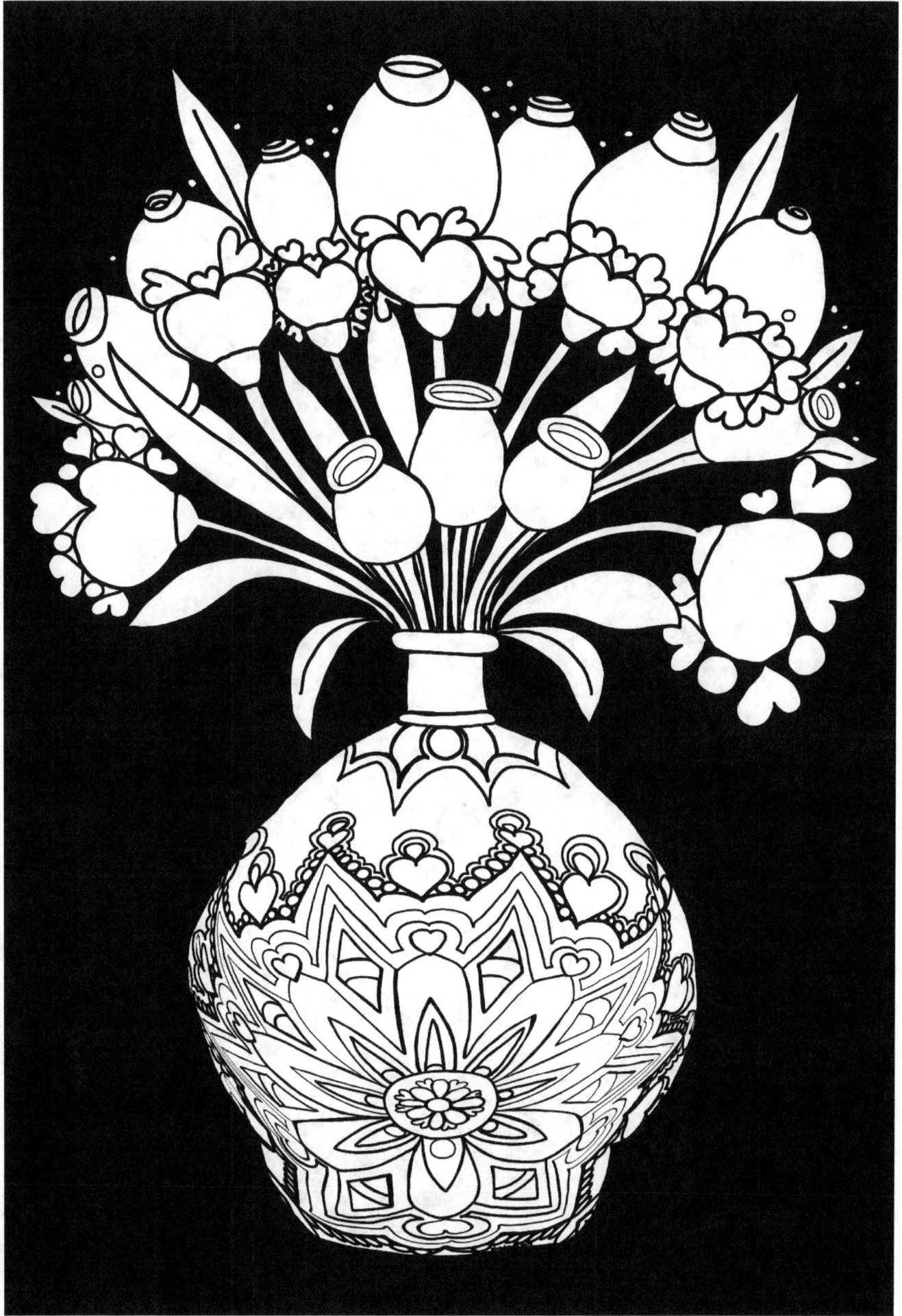

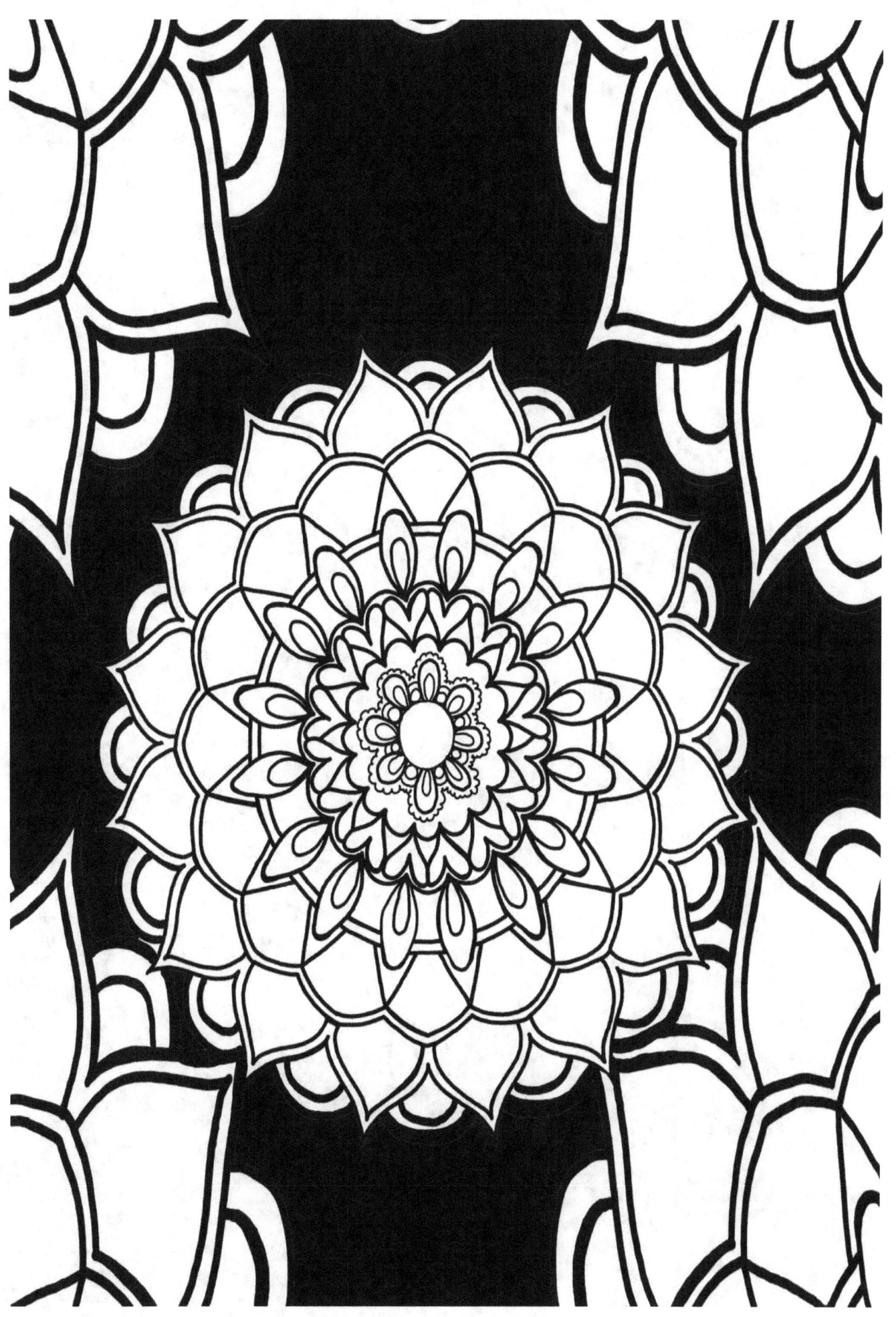

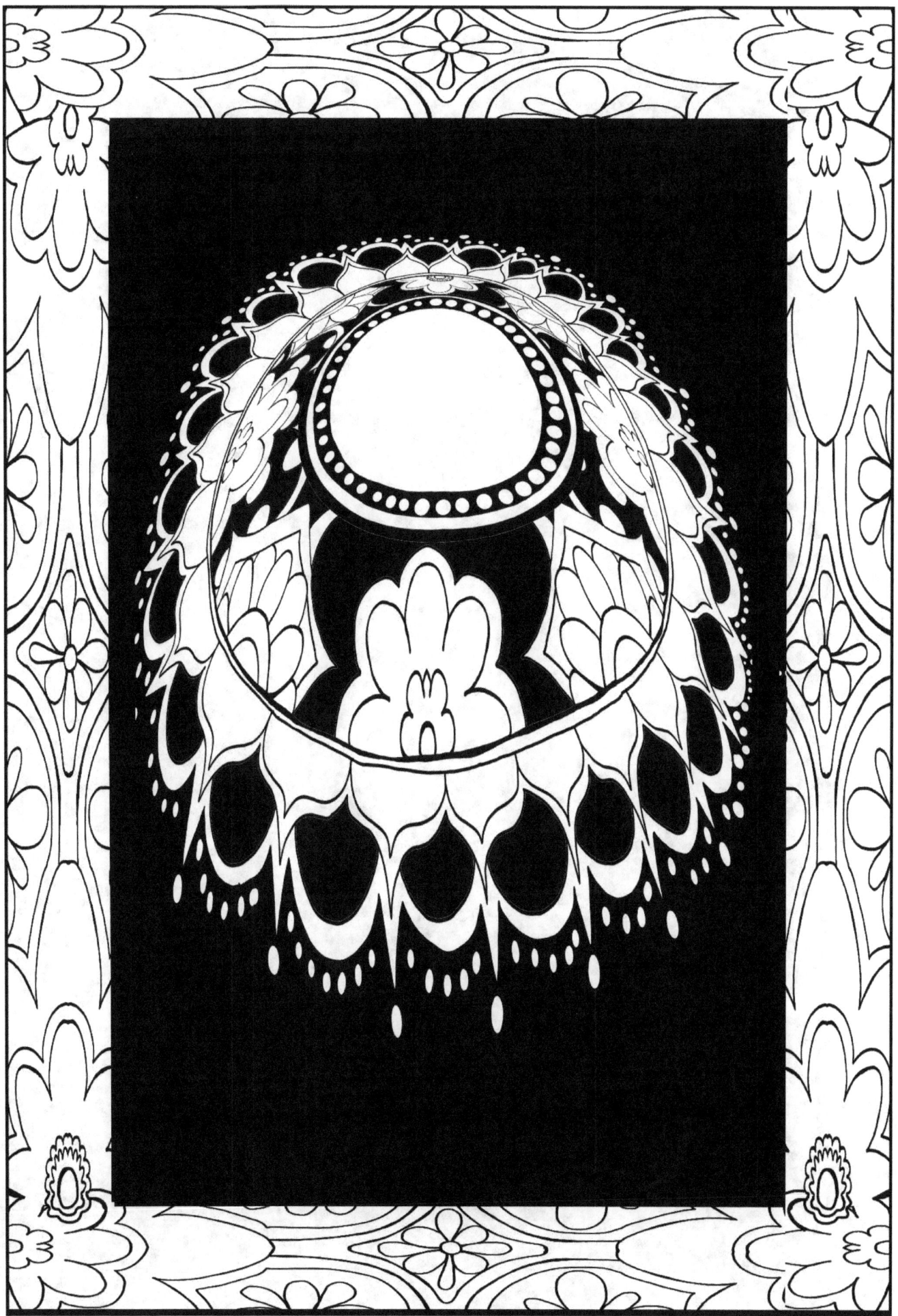

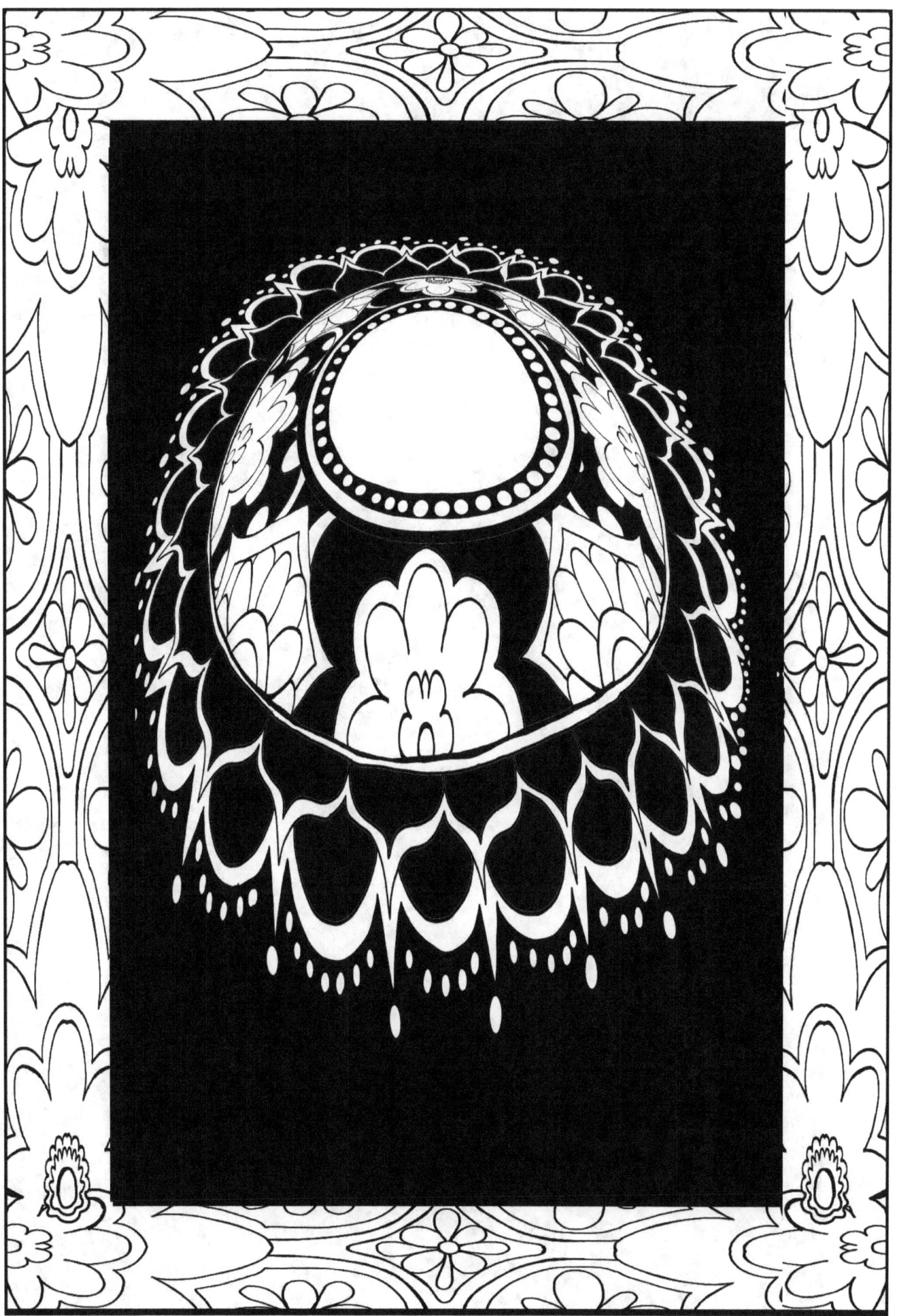

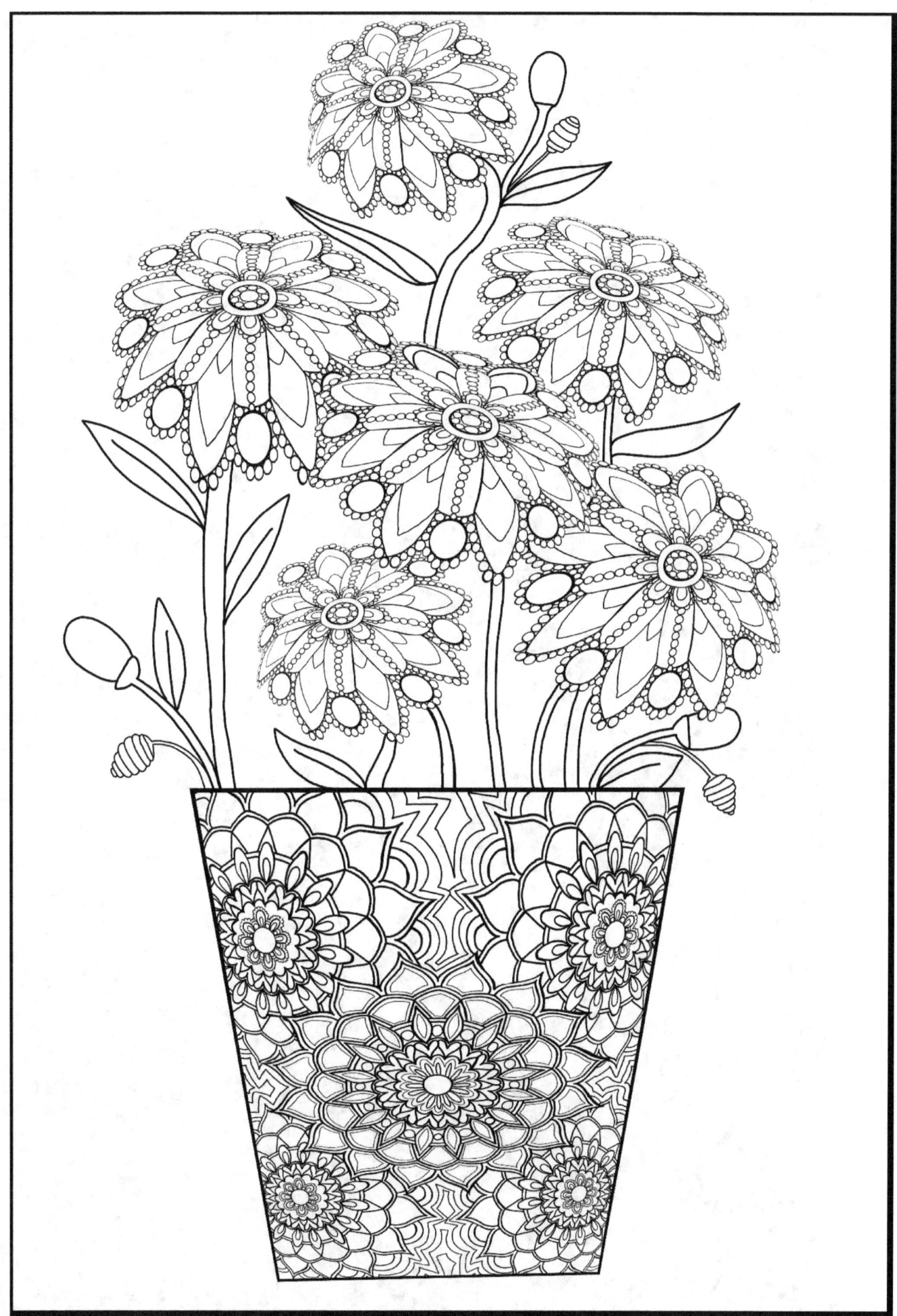

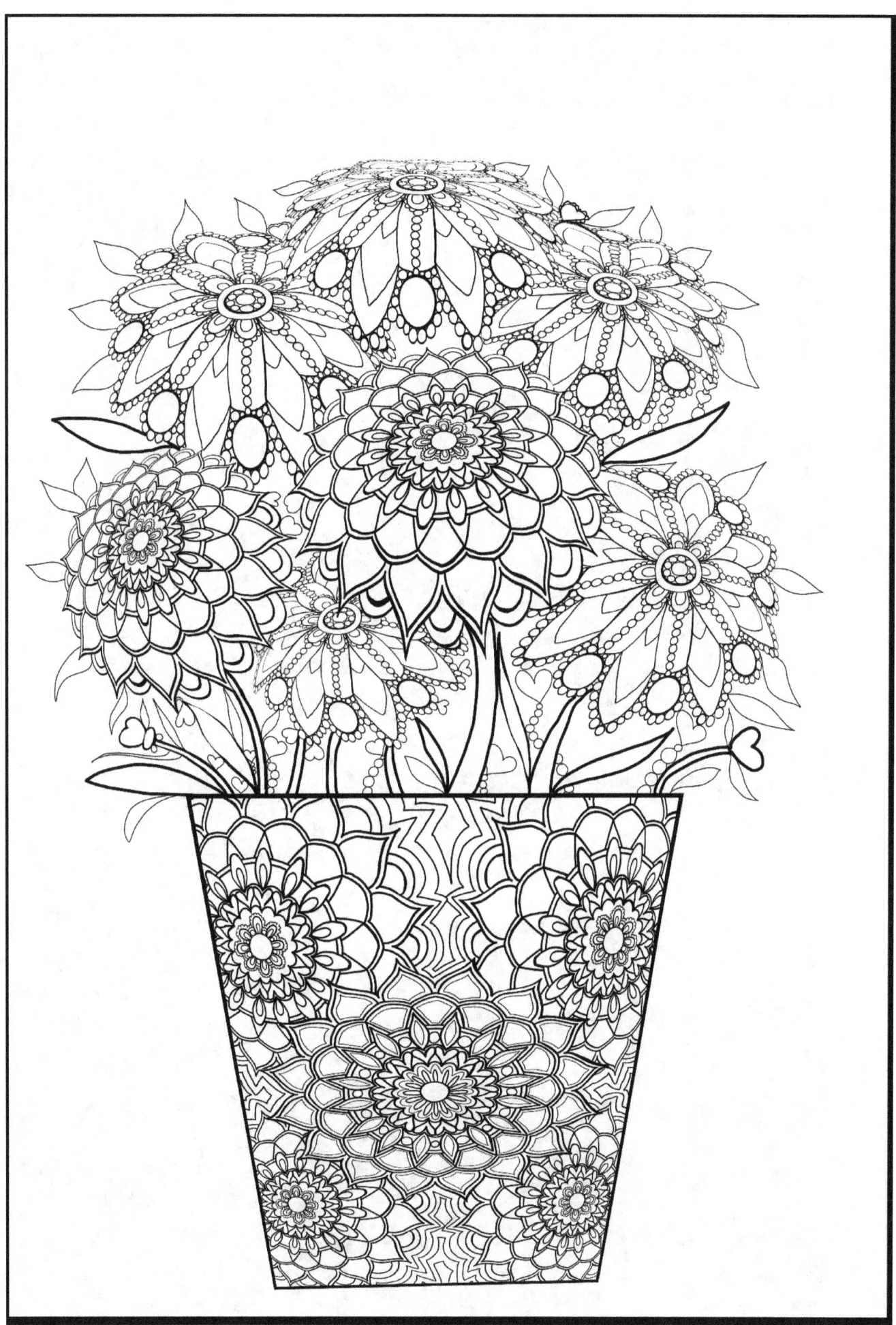

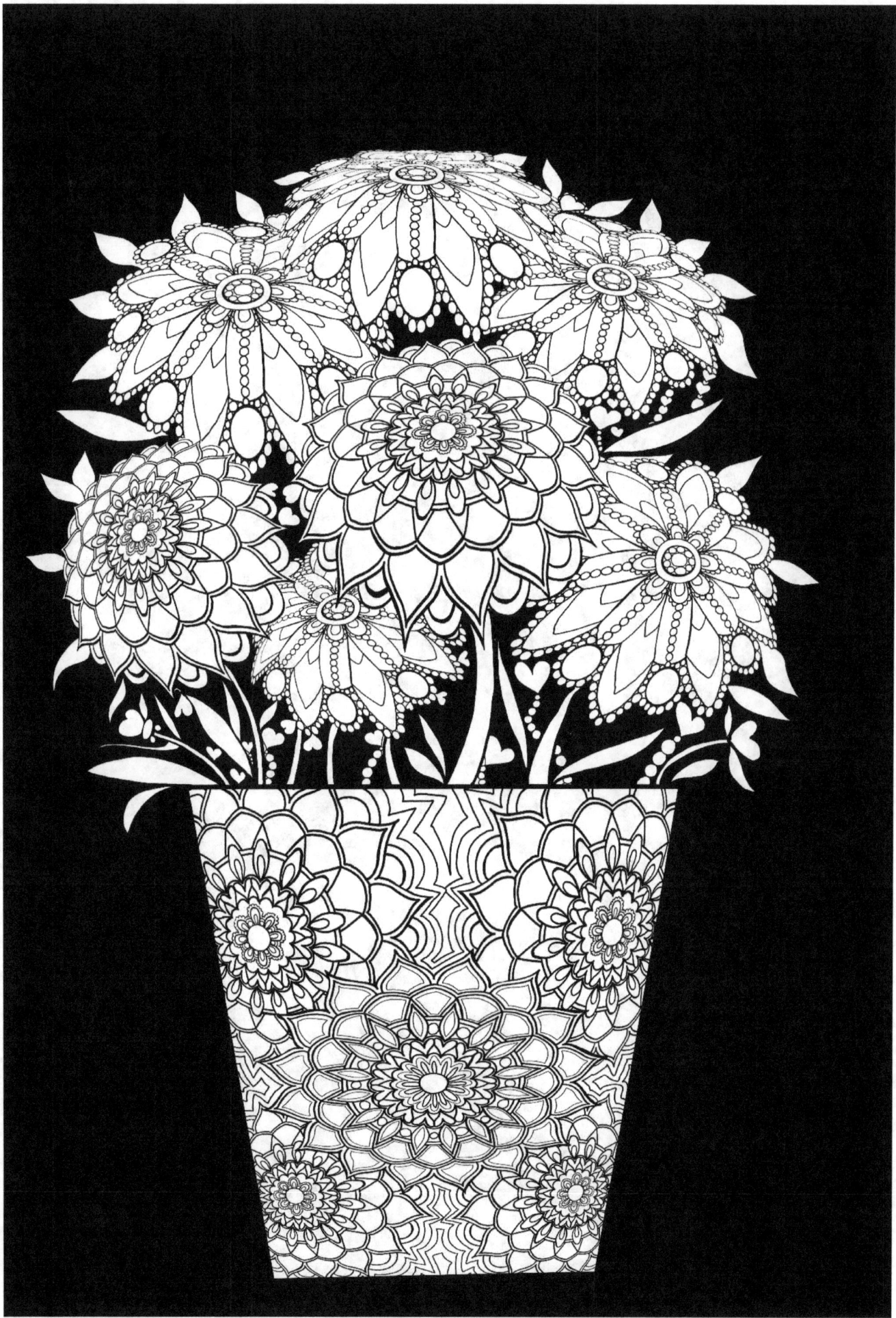

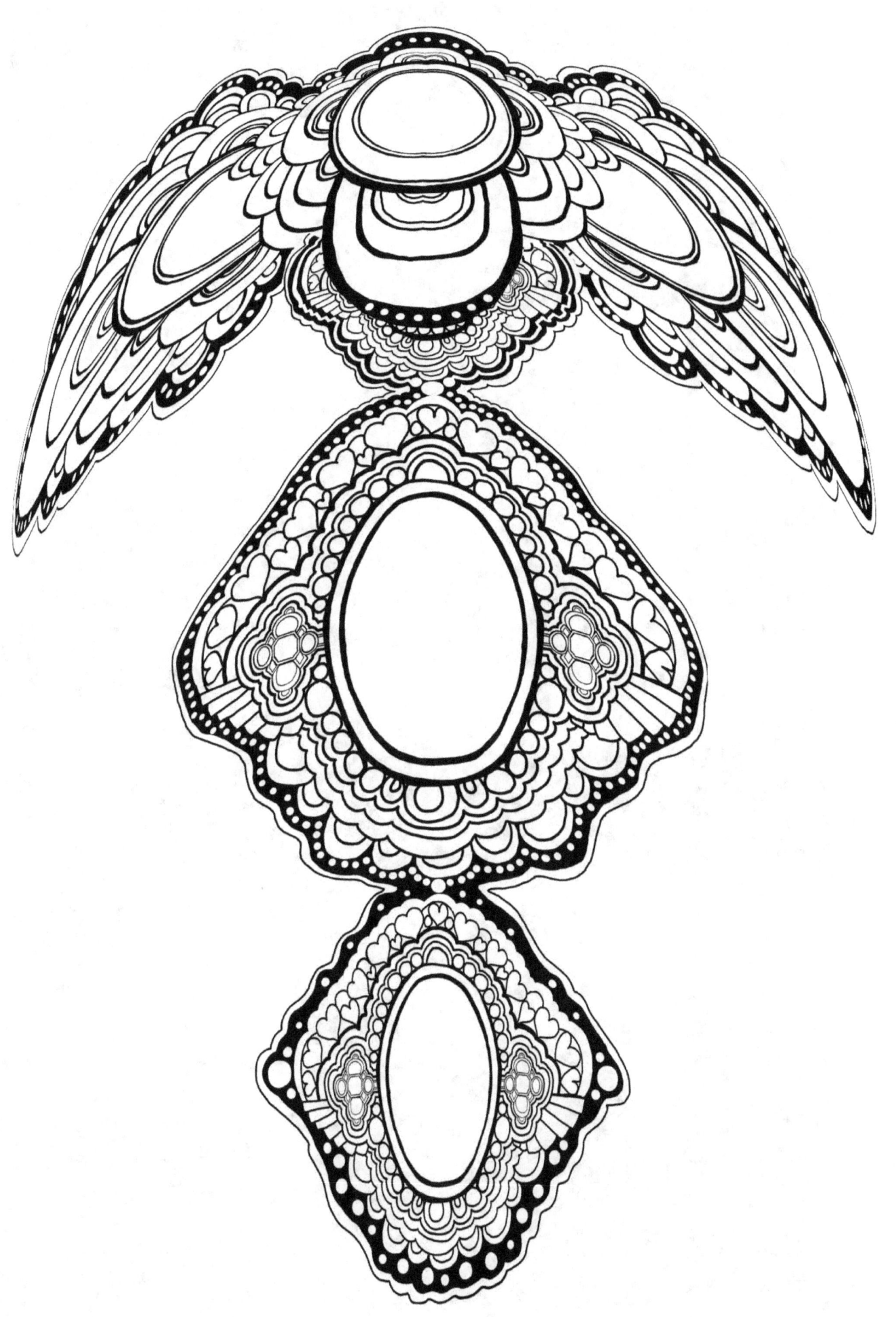

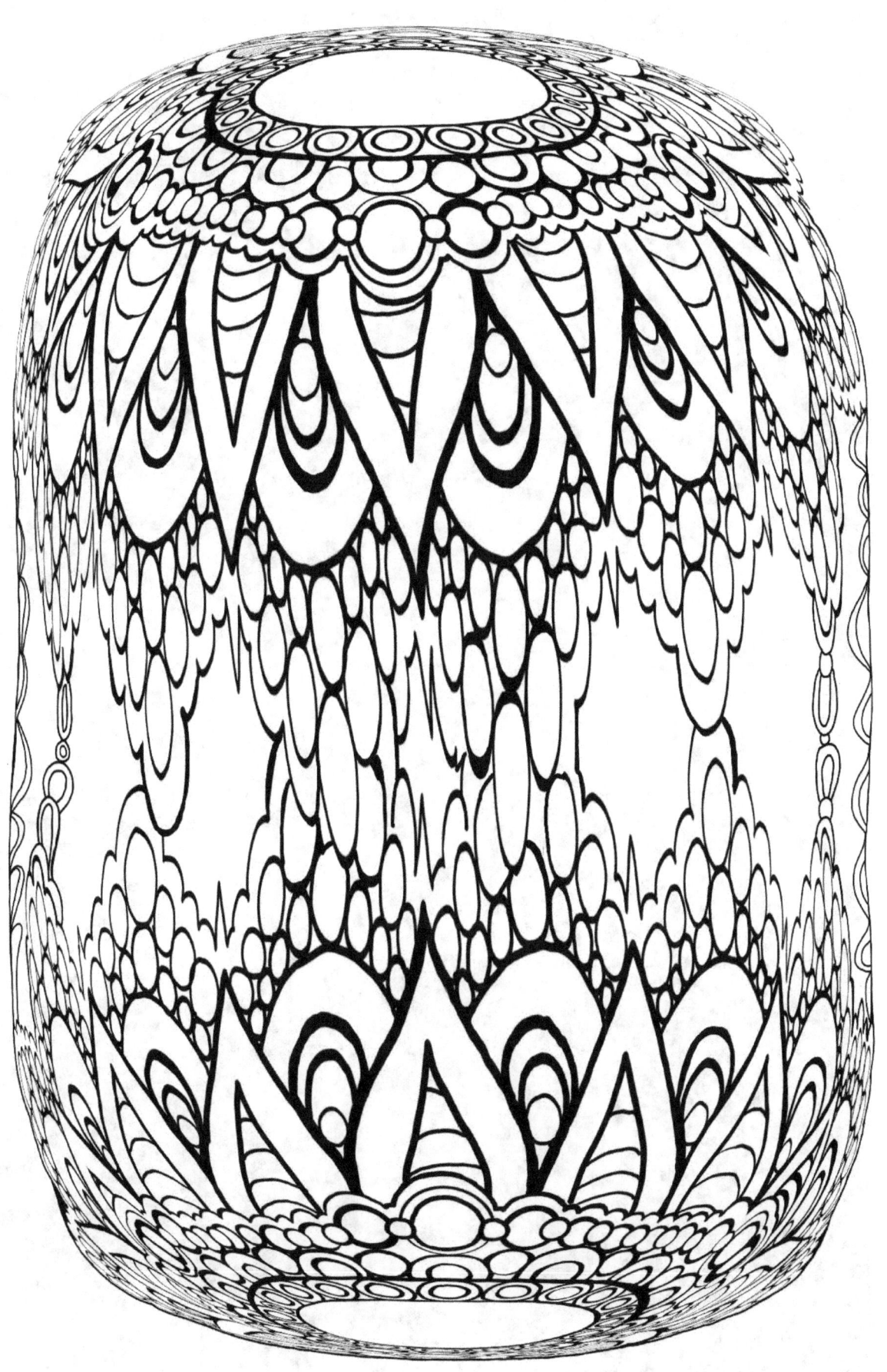

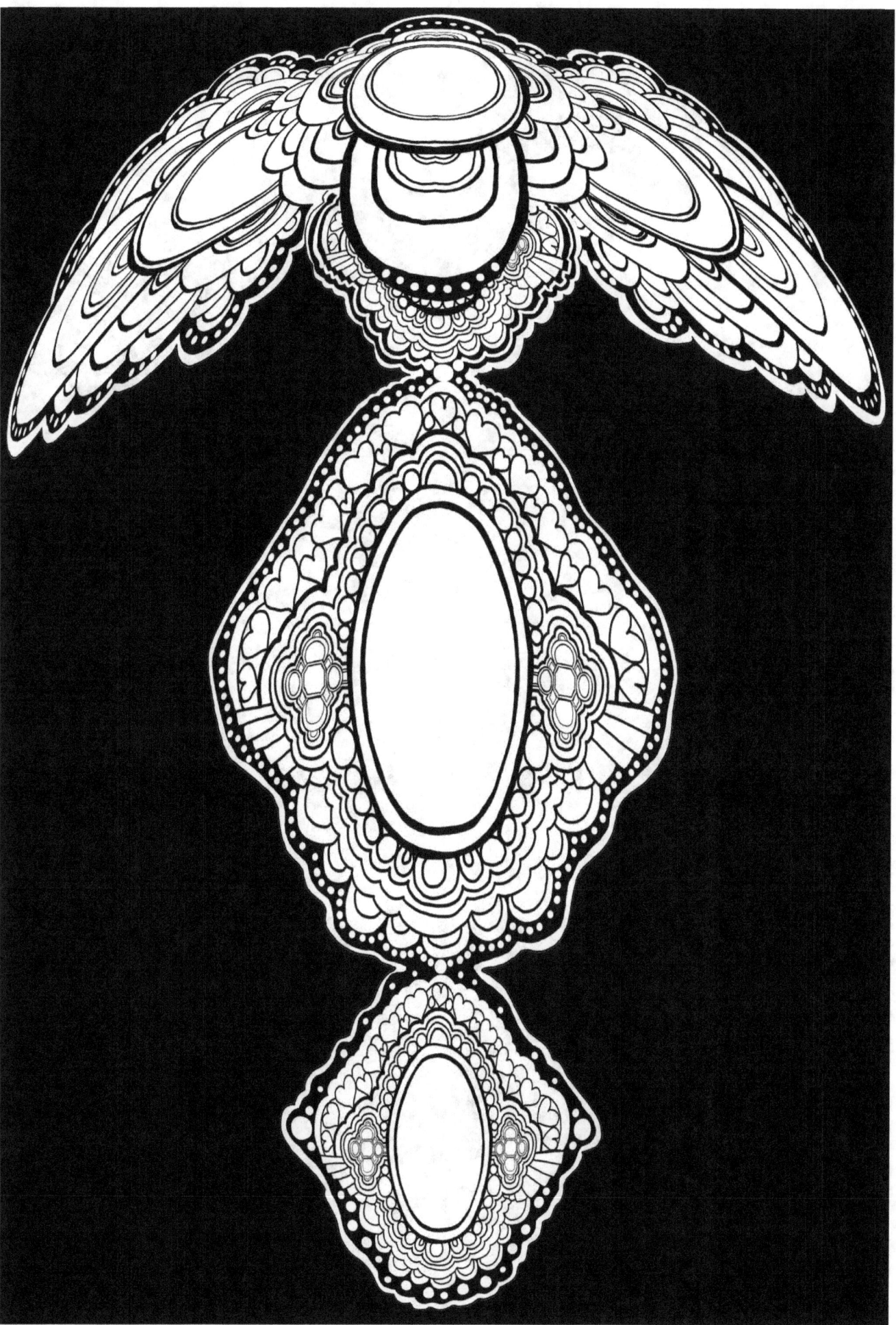

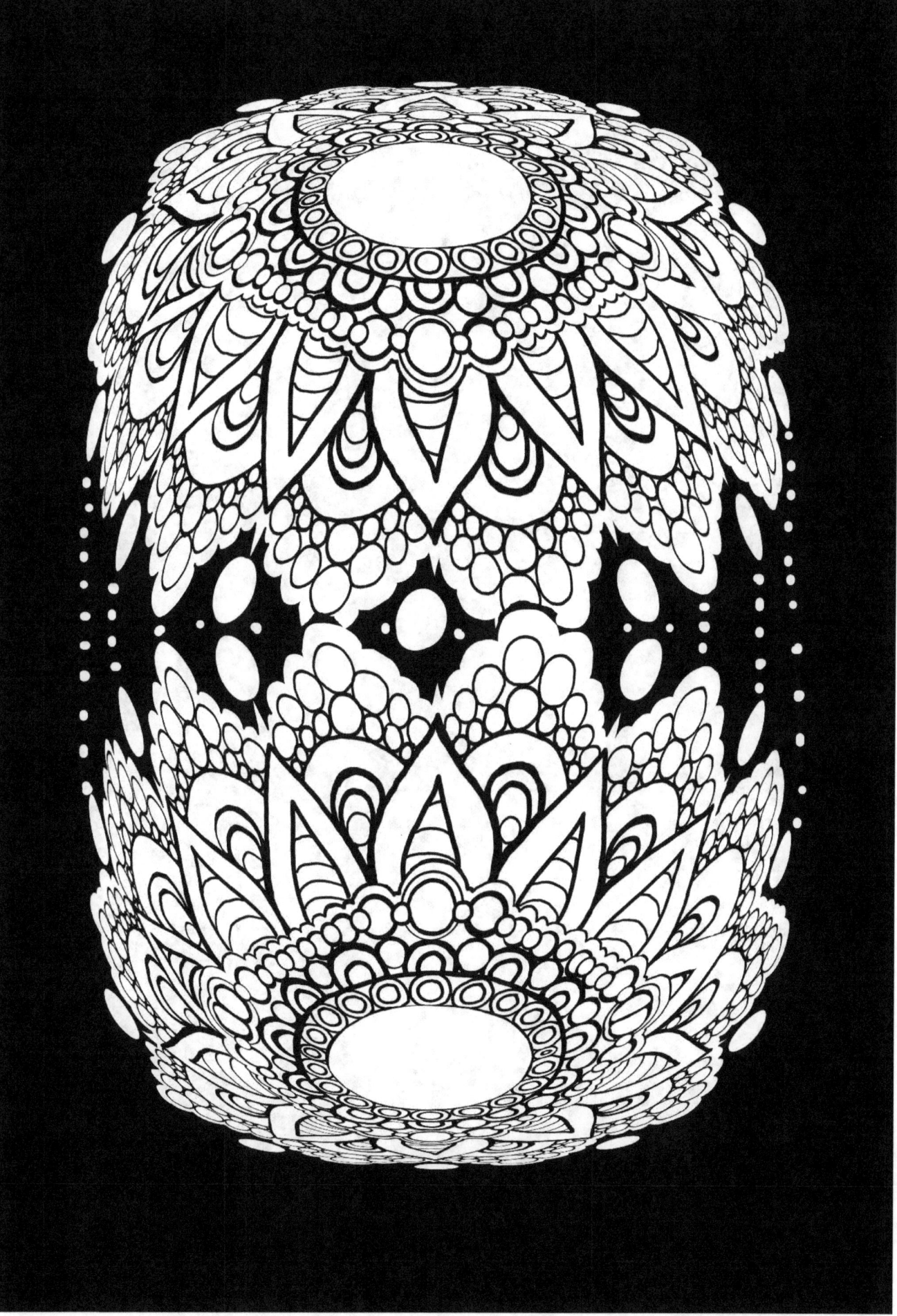

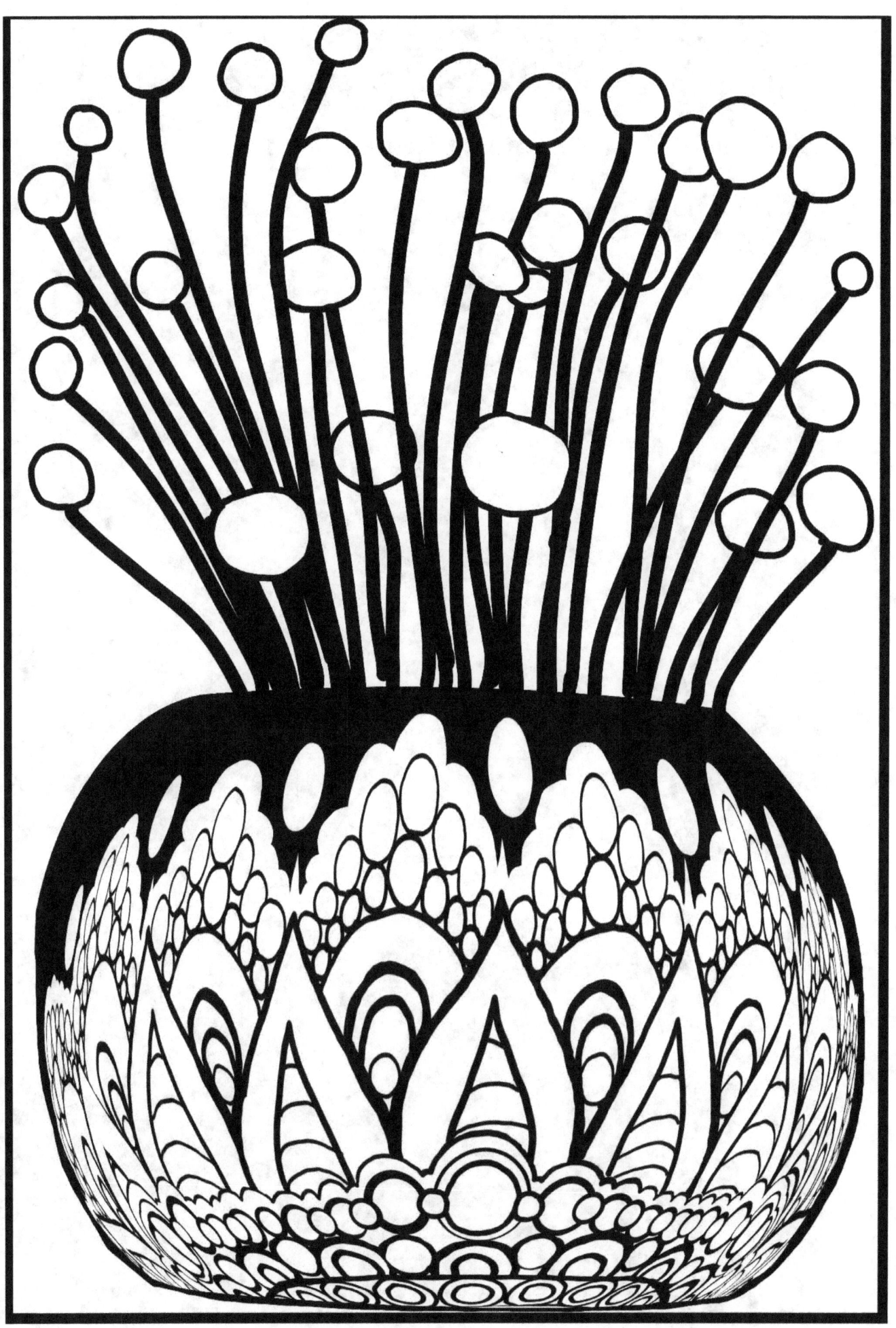

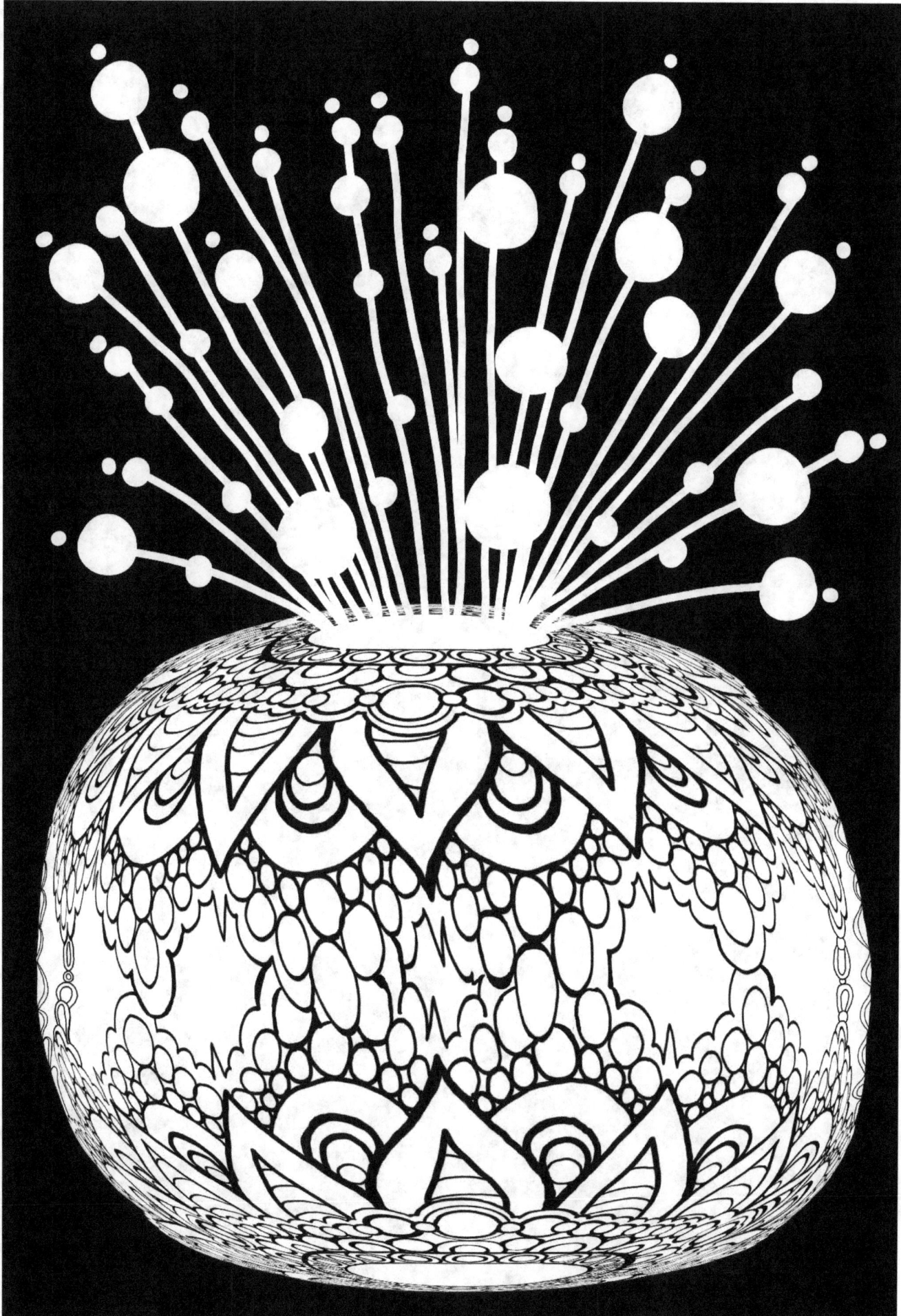

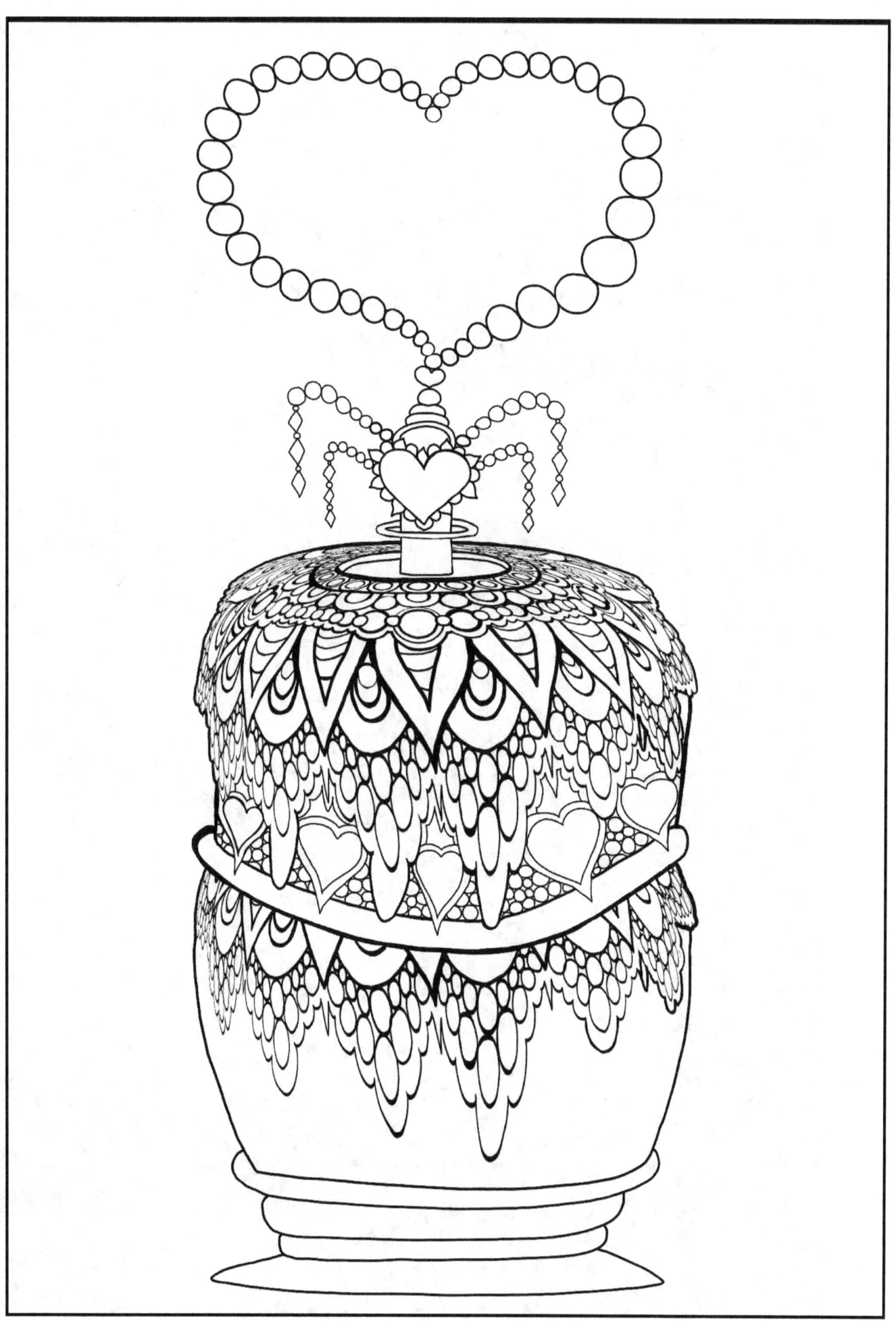

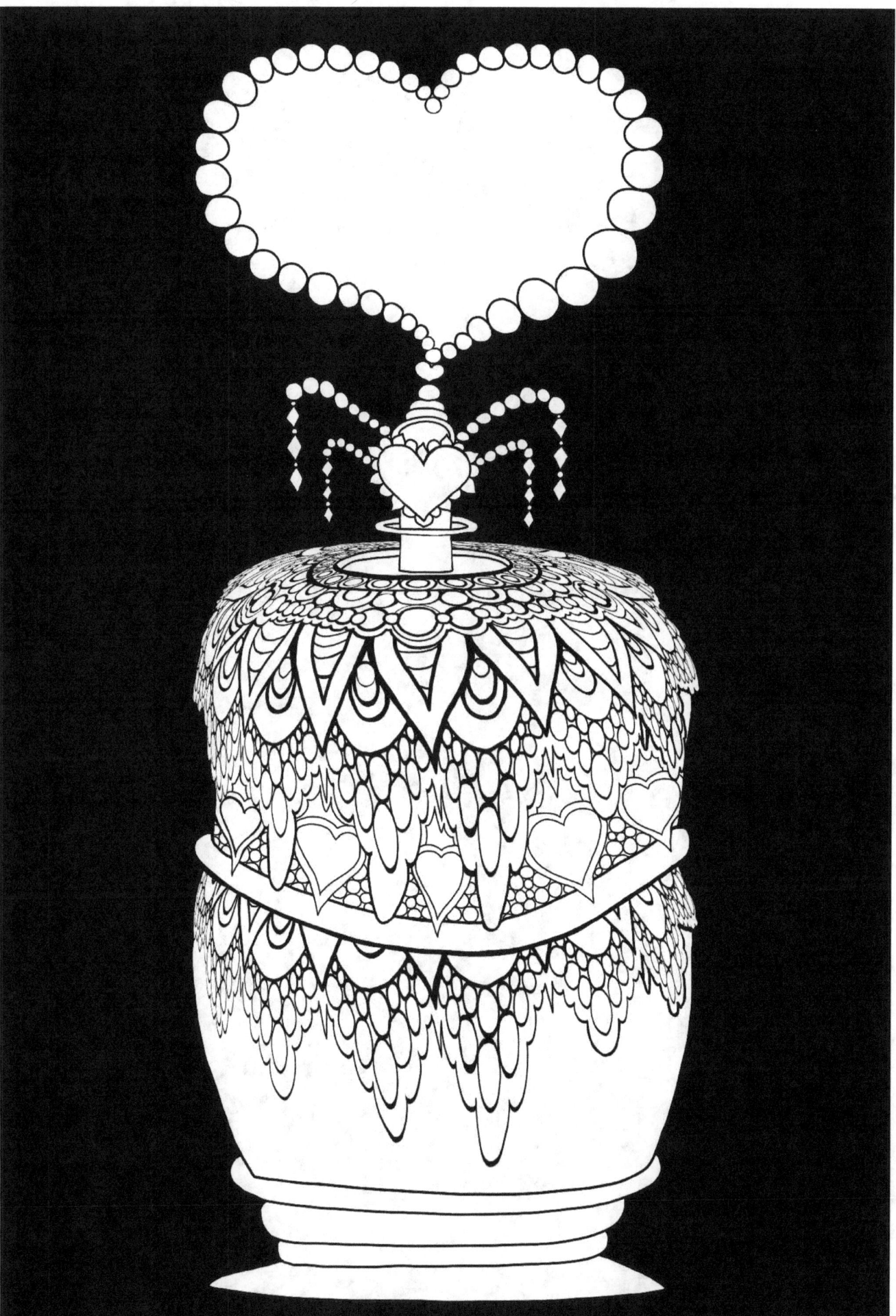

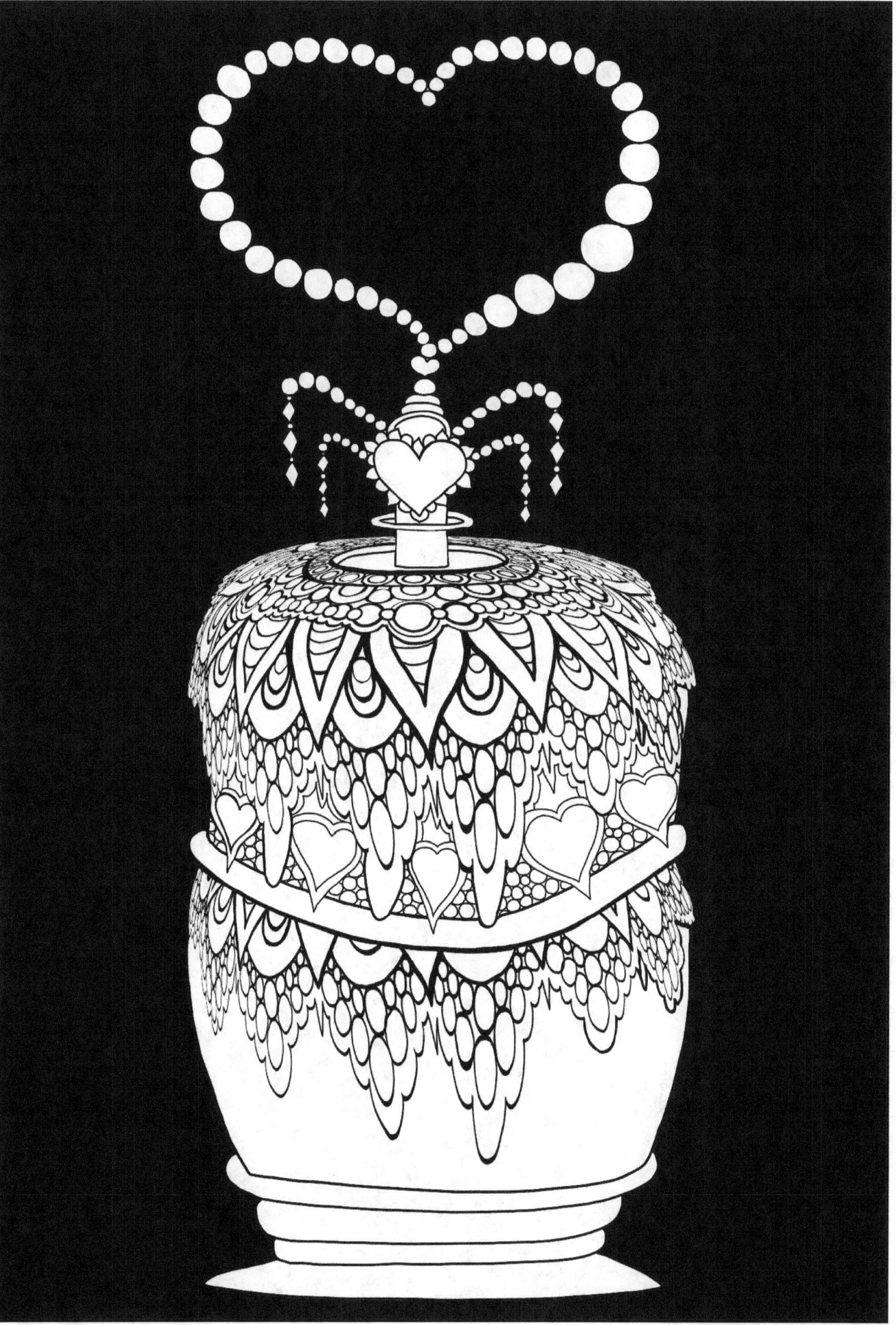

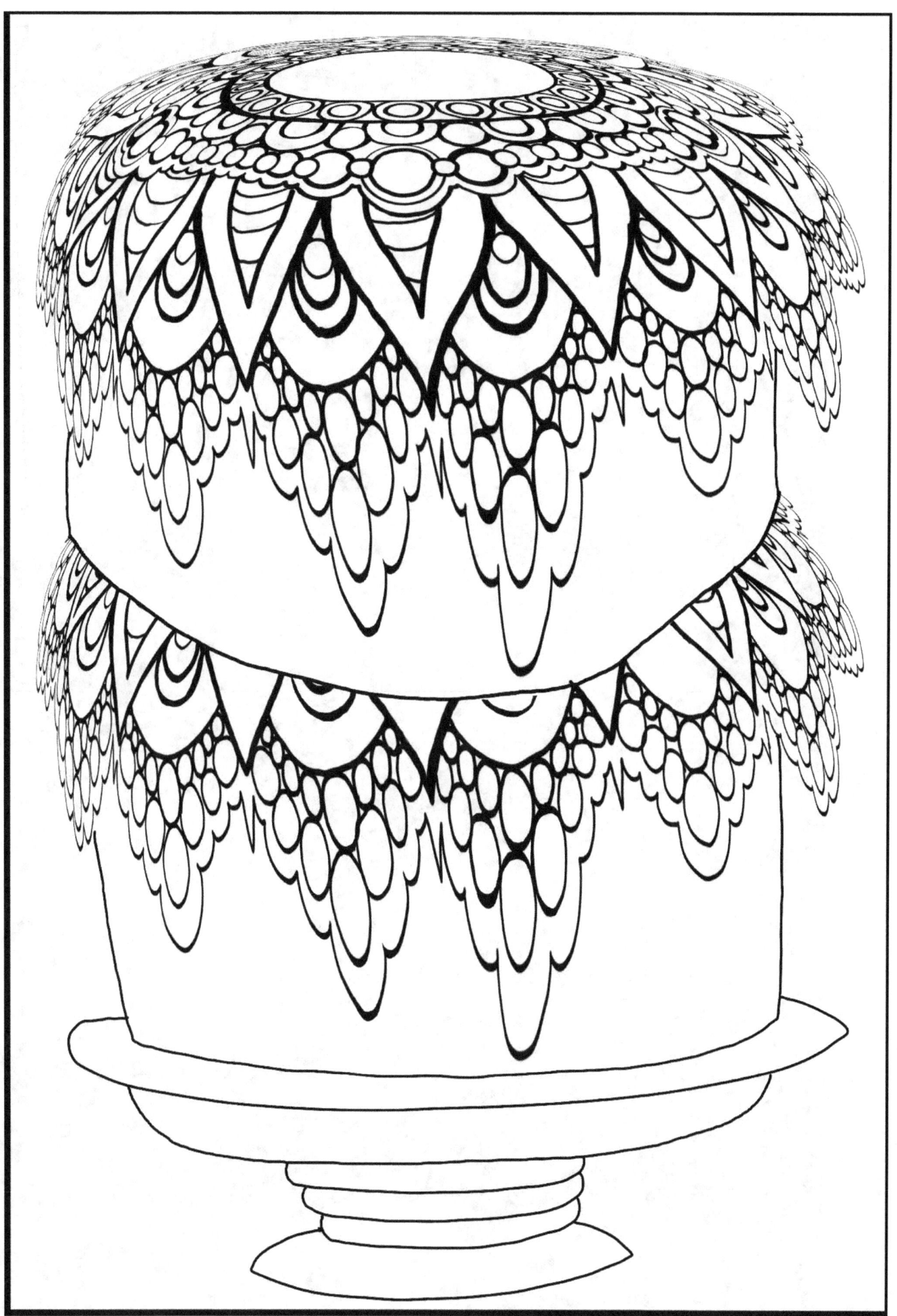

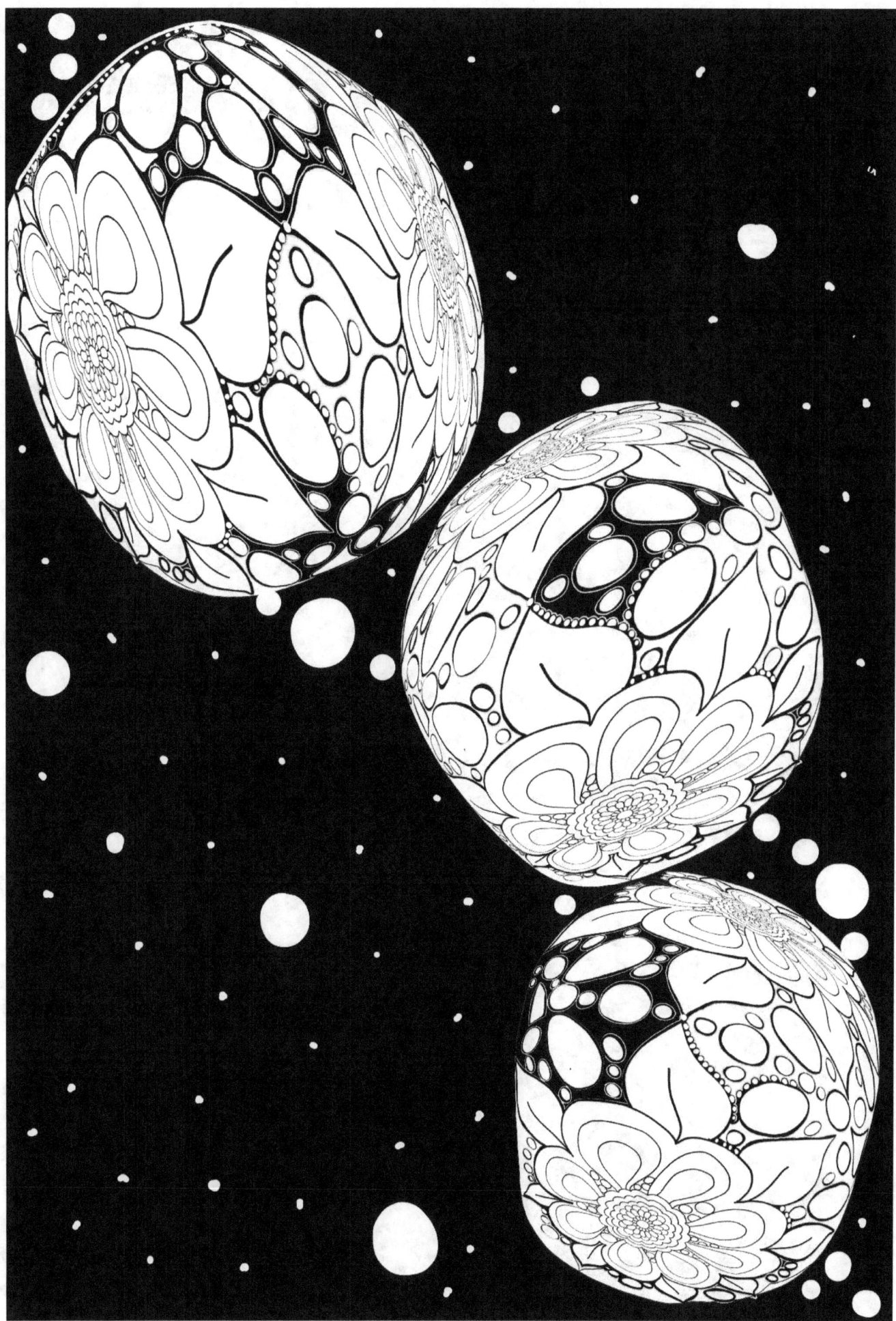

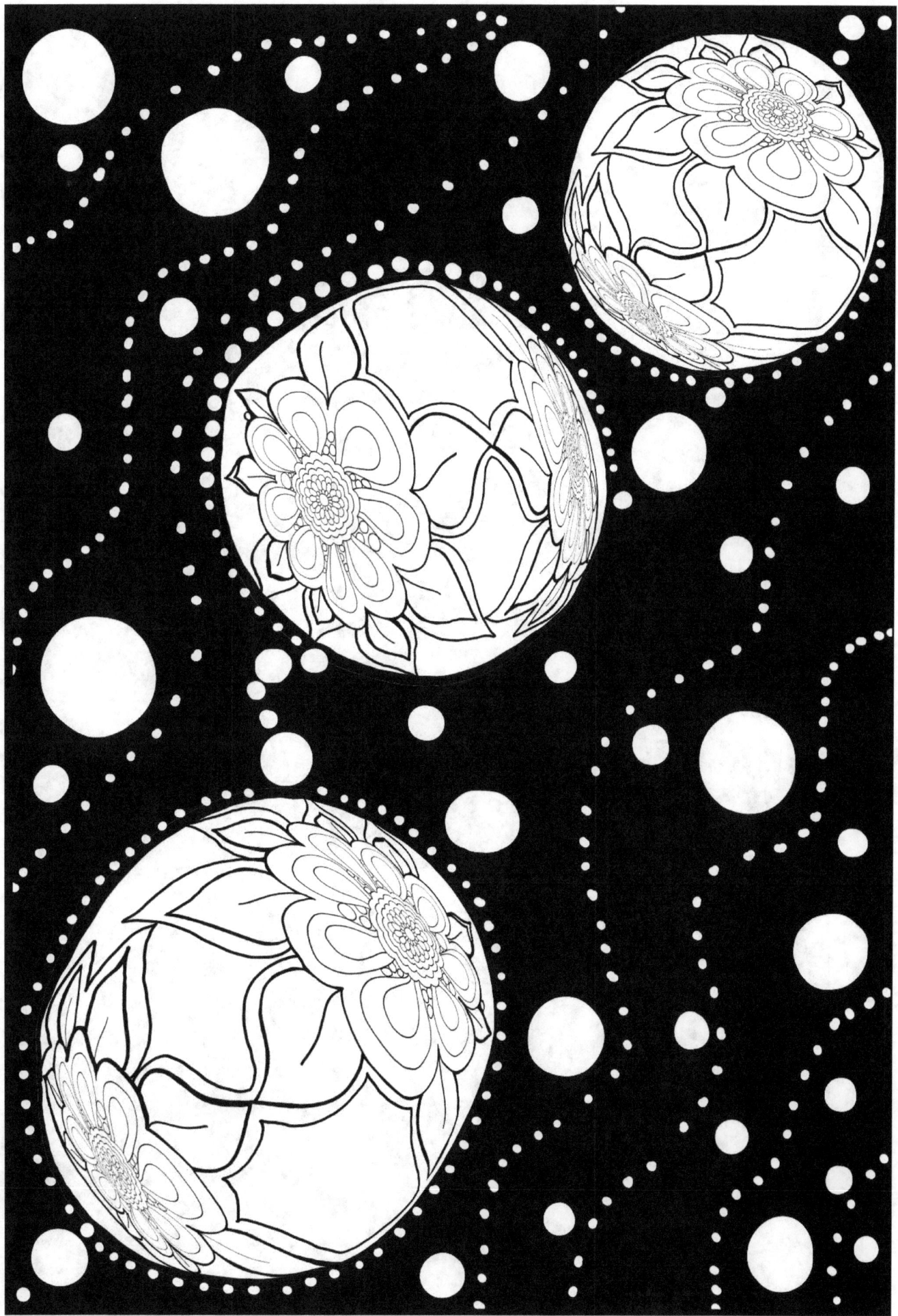

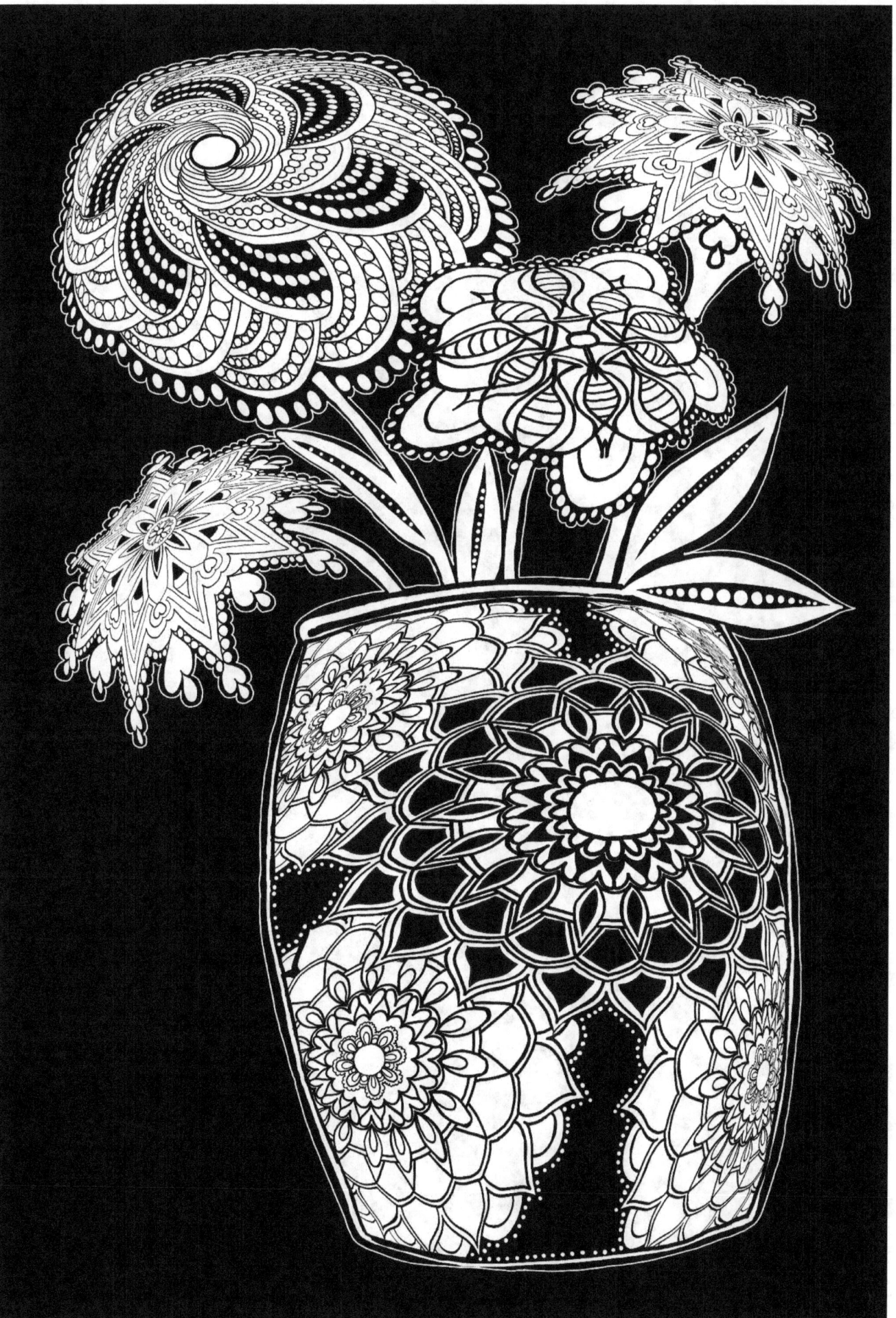

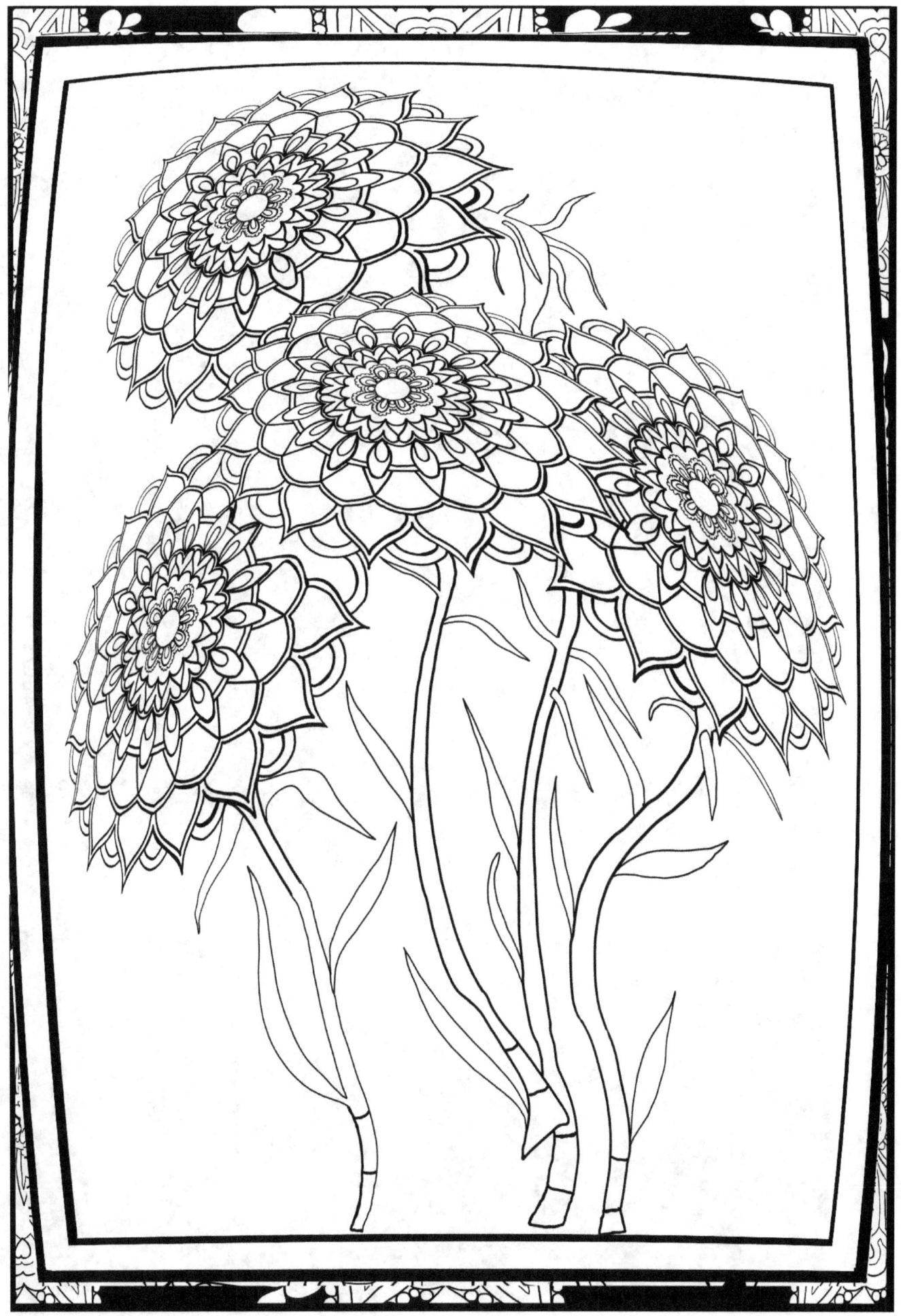

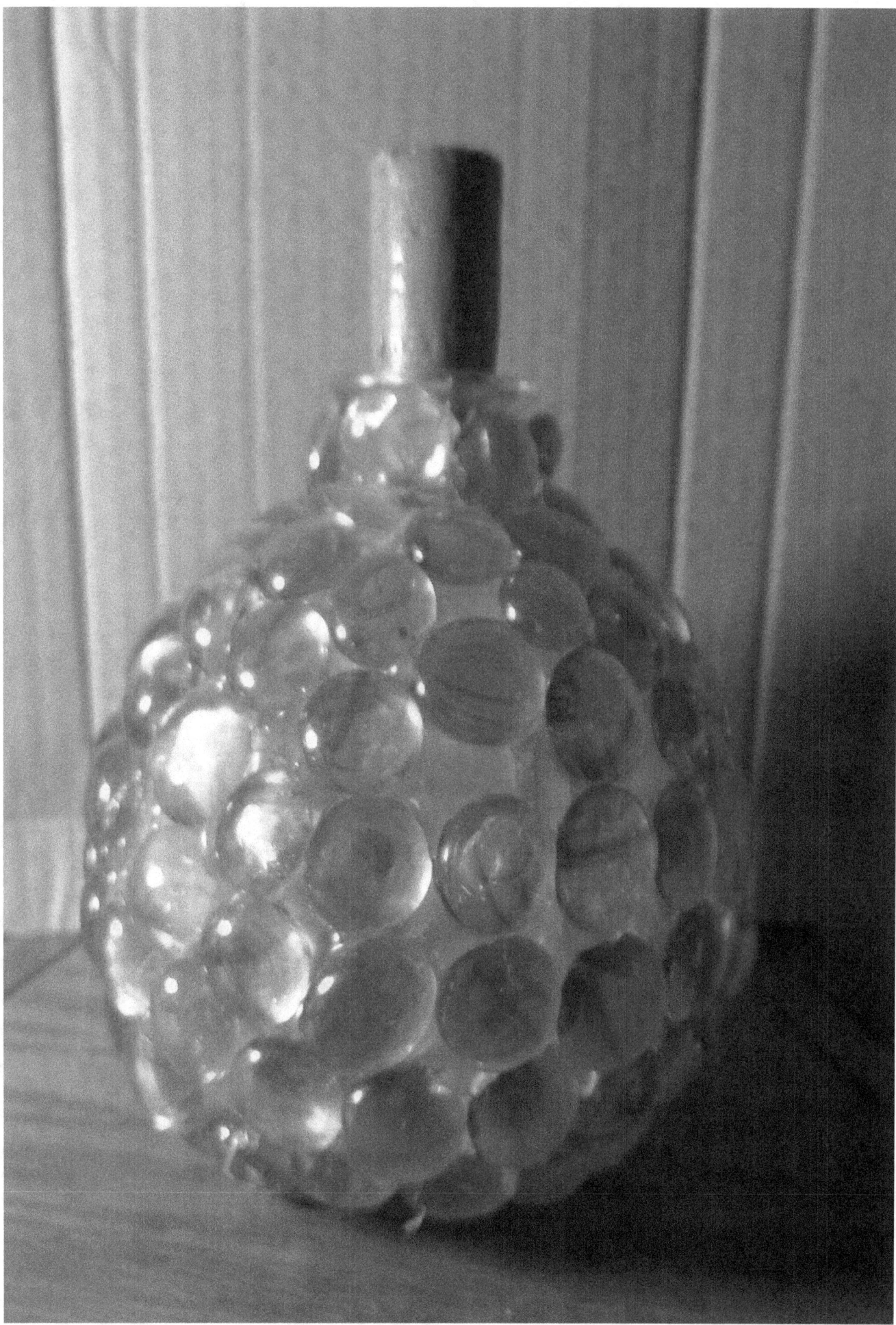

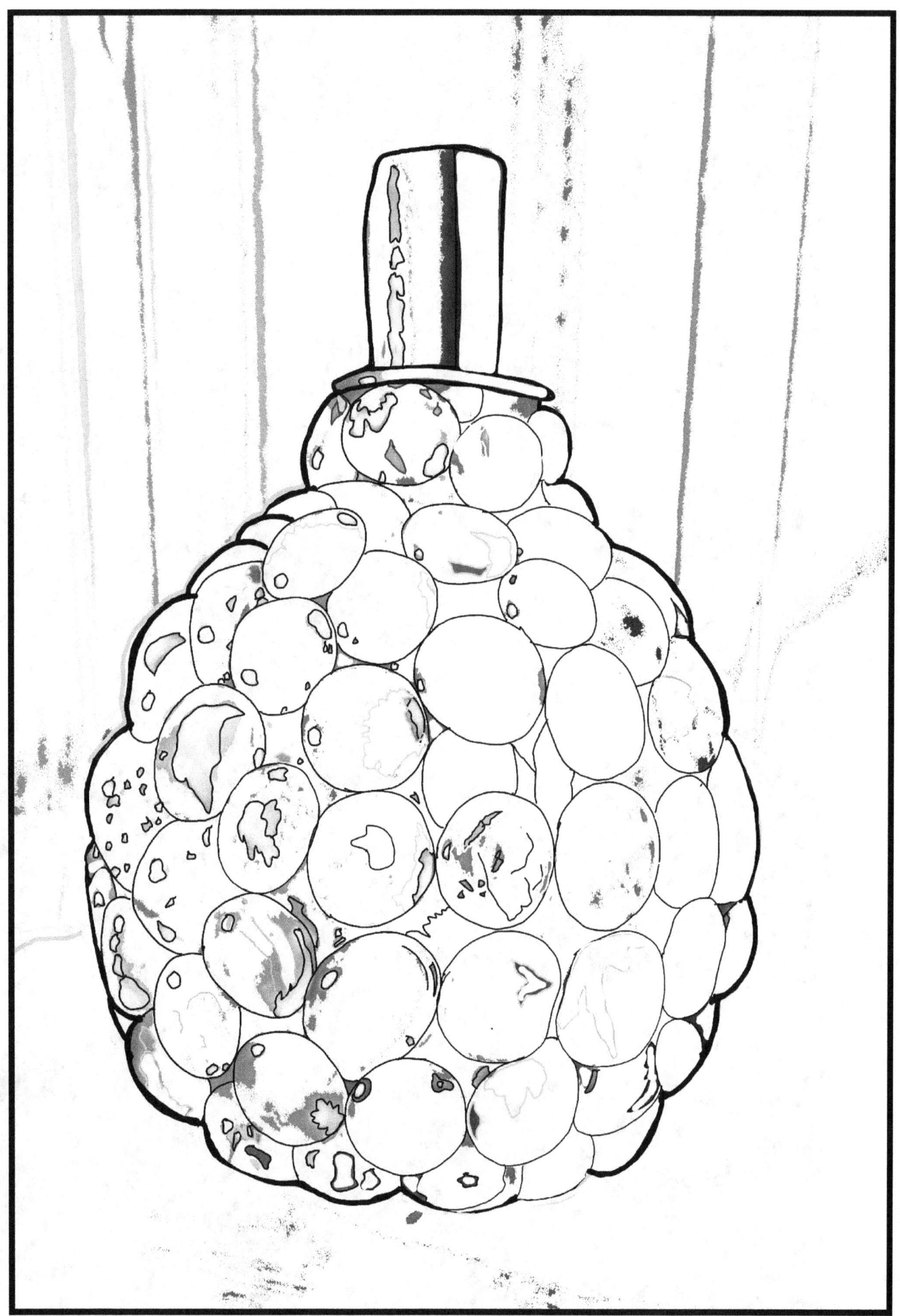

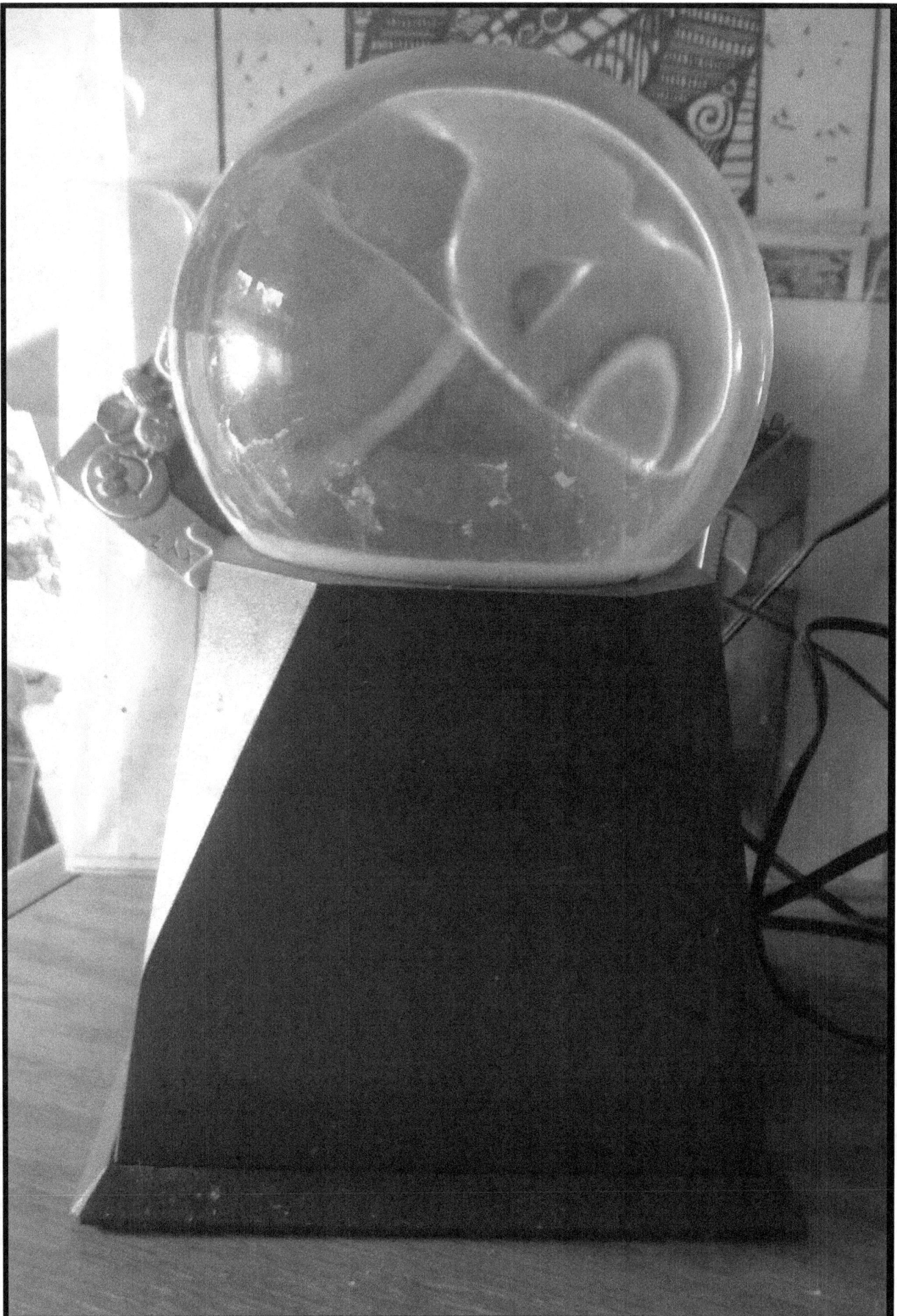

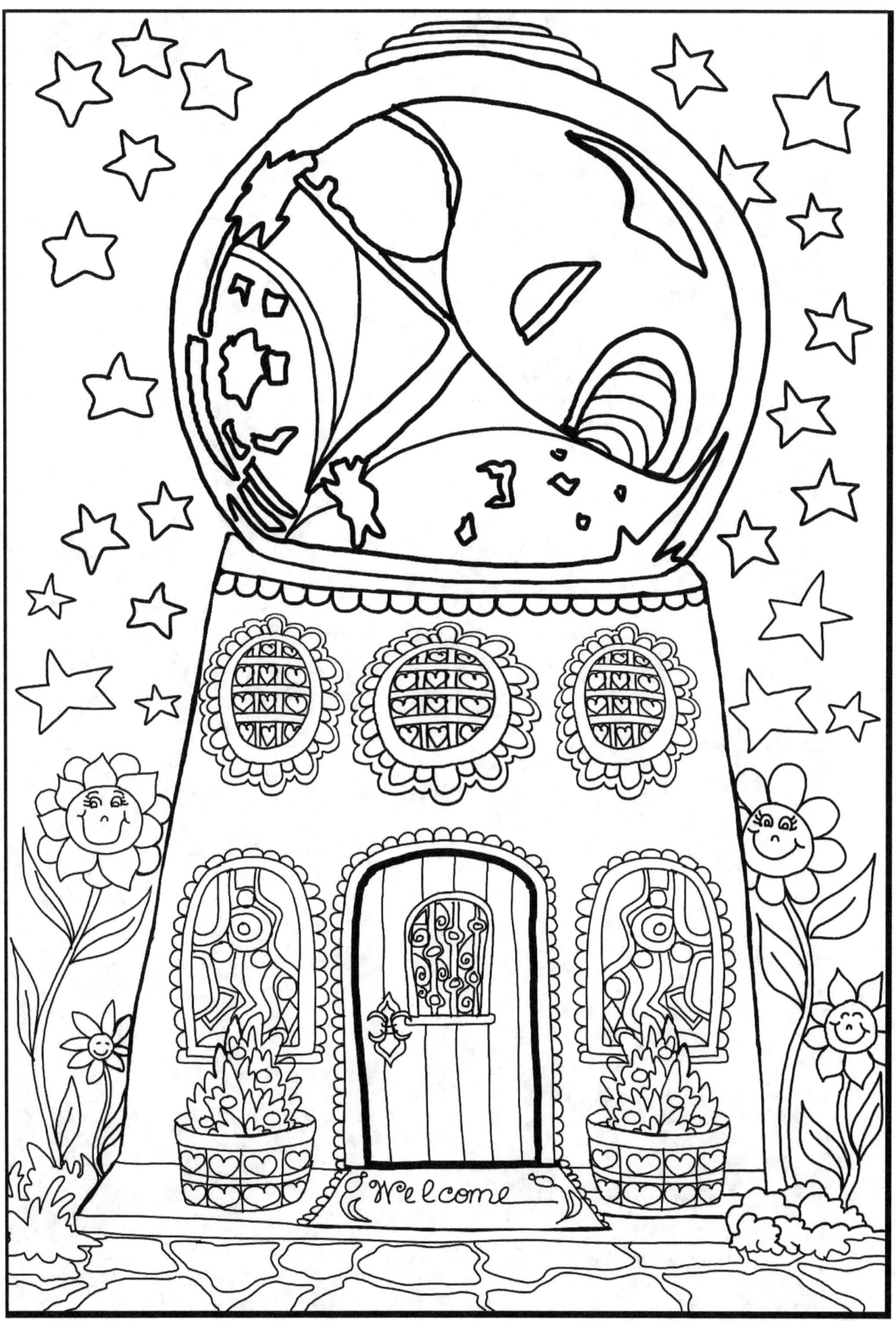

Welcome

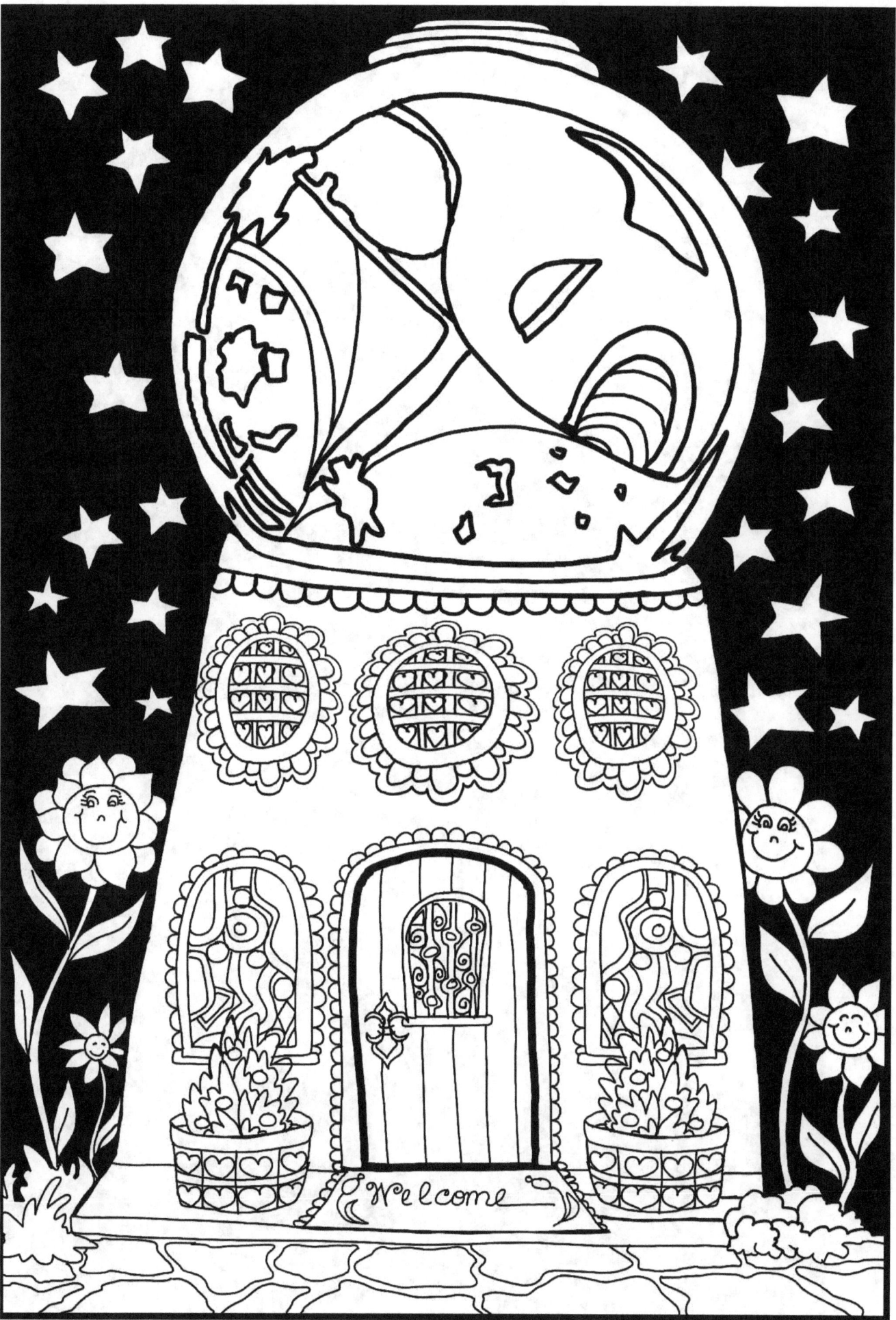

Welcome

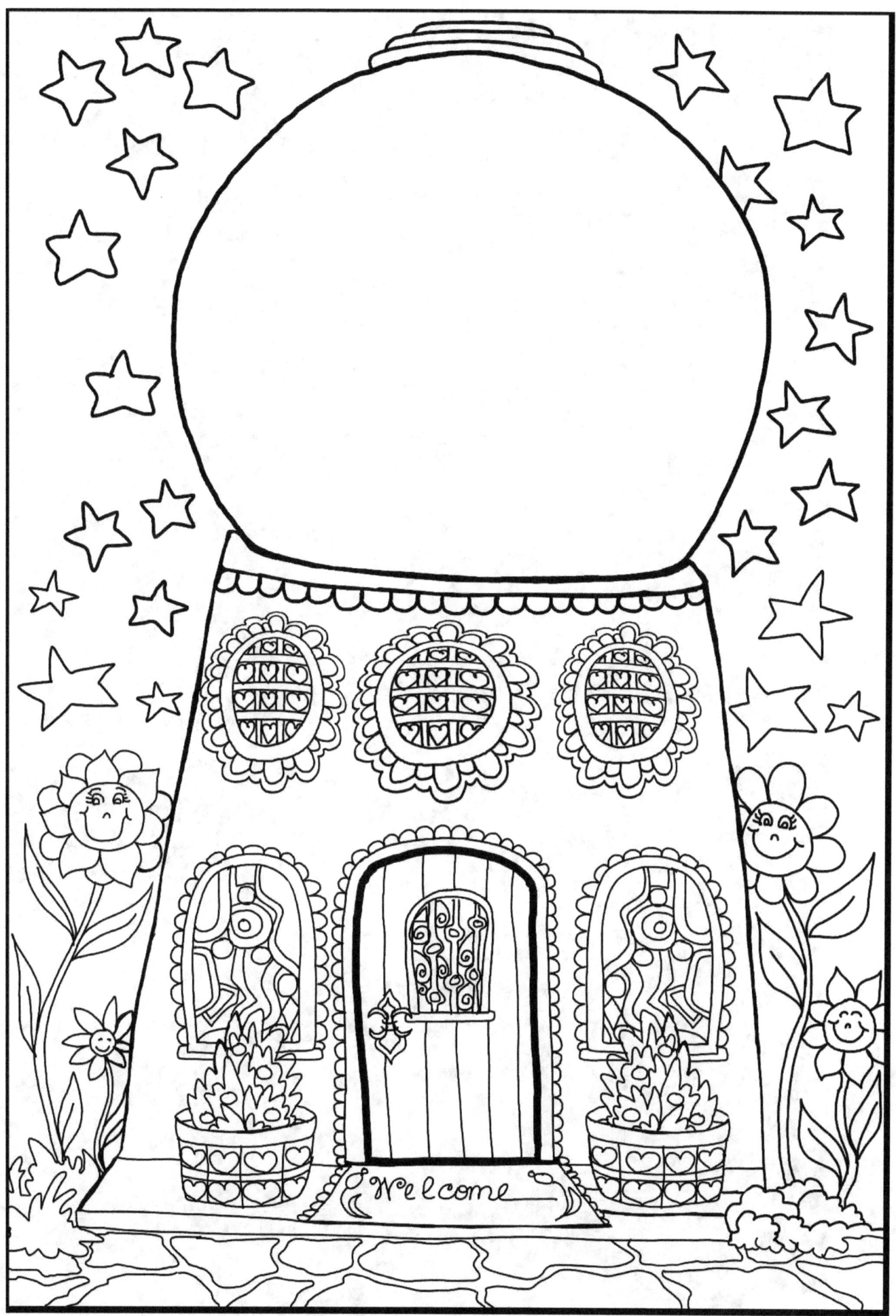

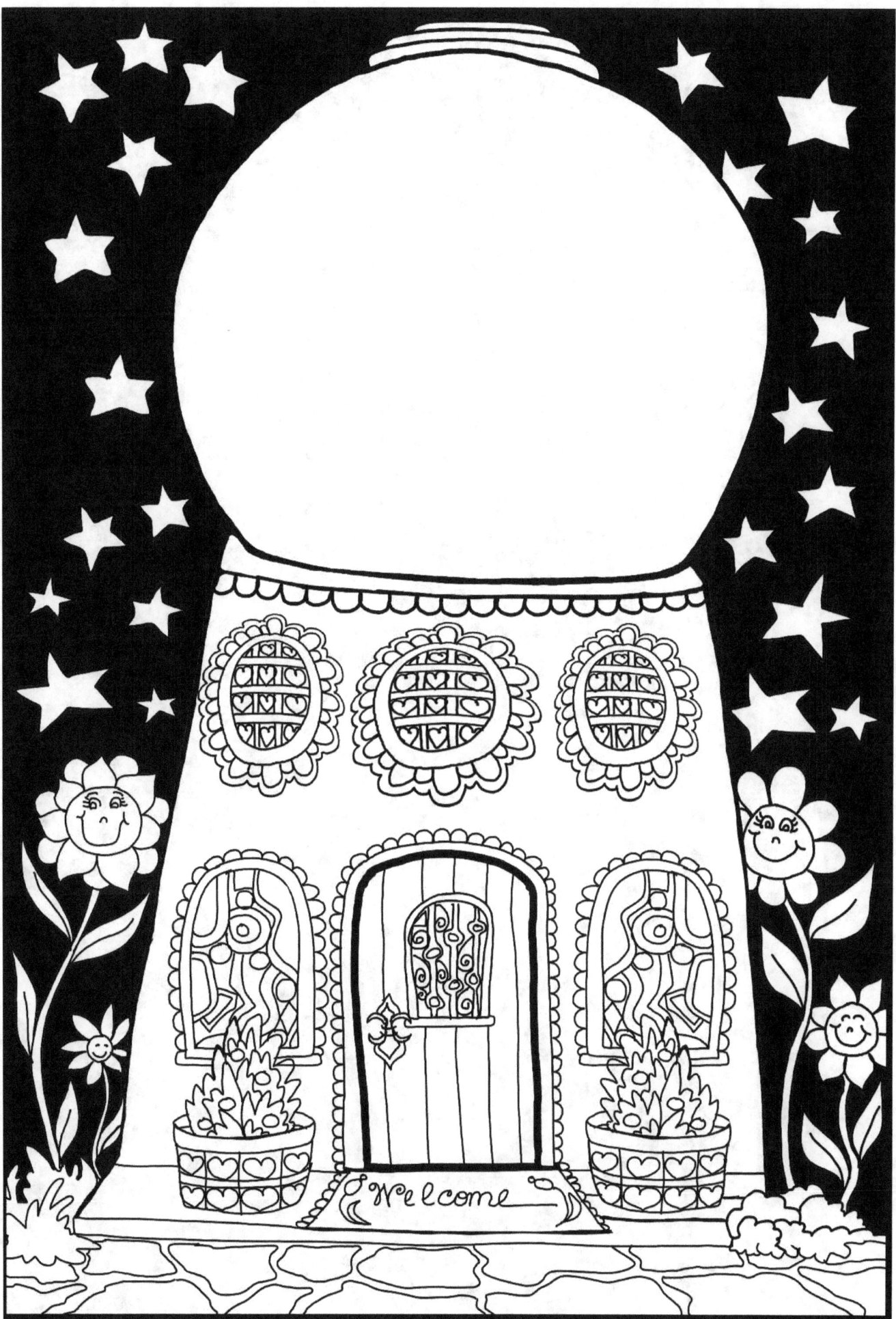

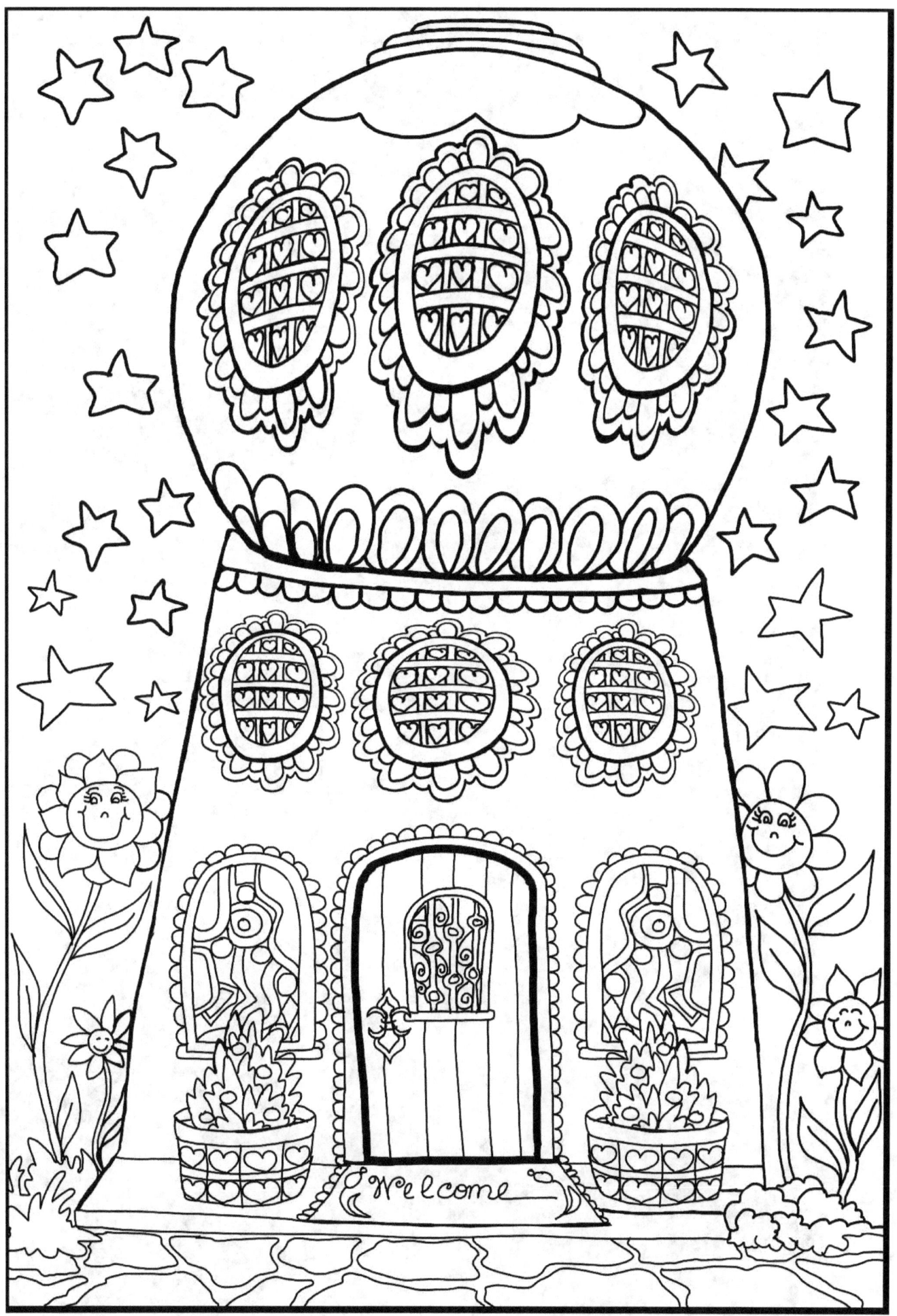

Welcome

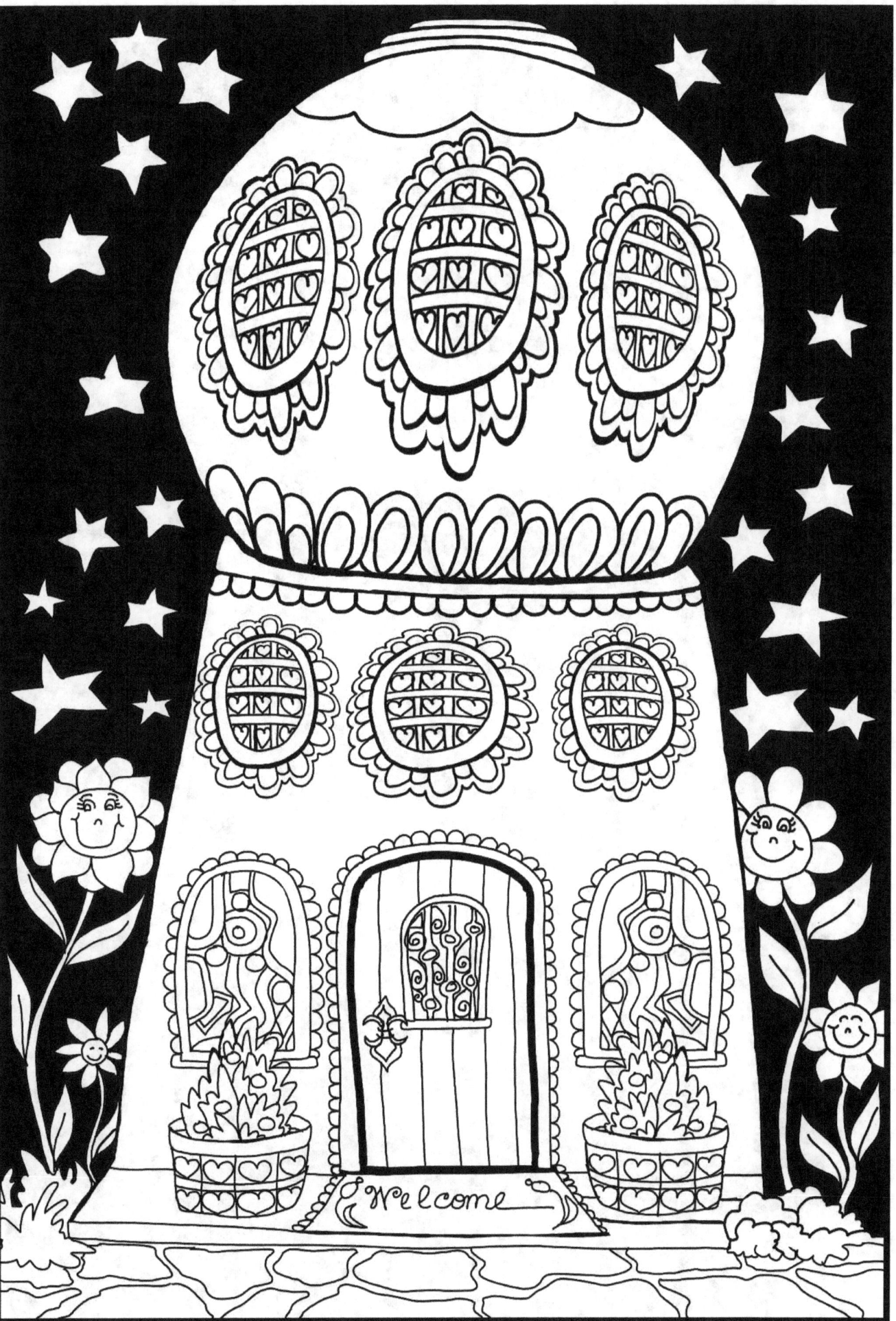

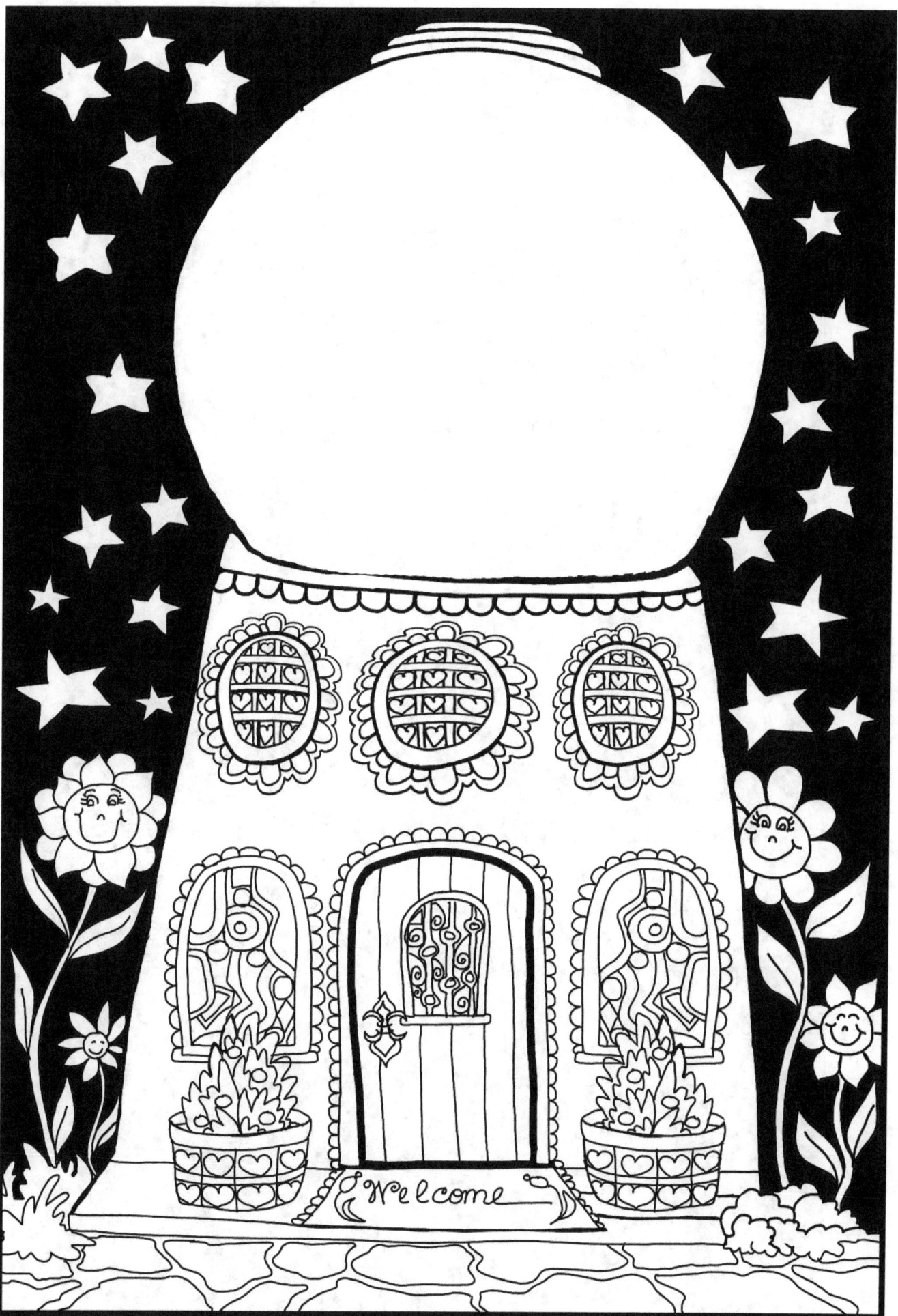

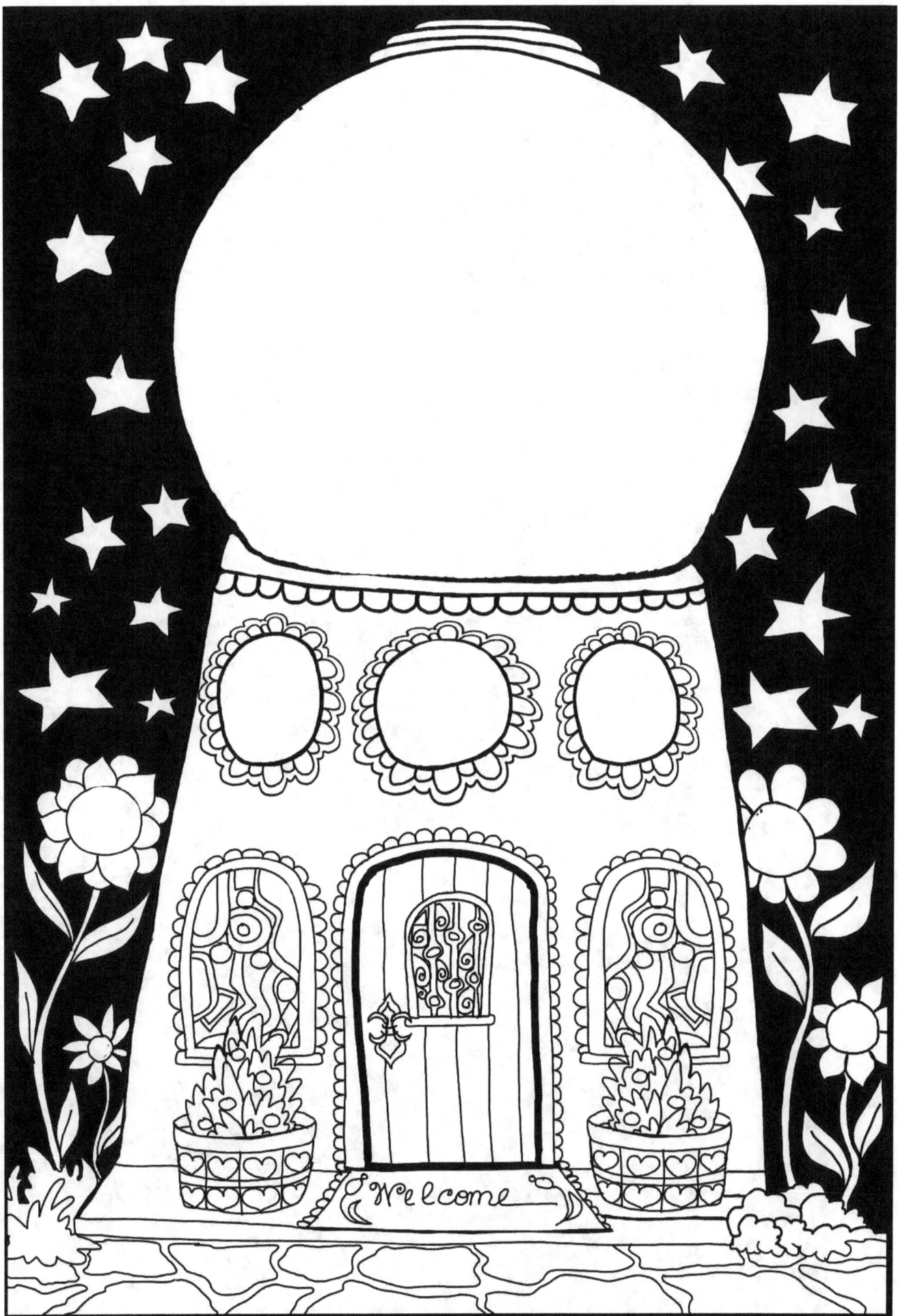

Welcome

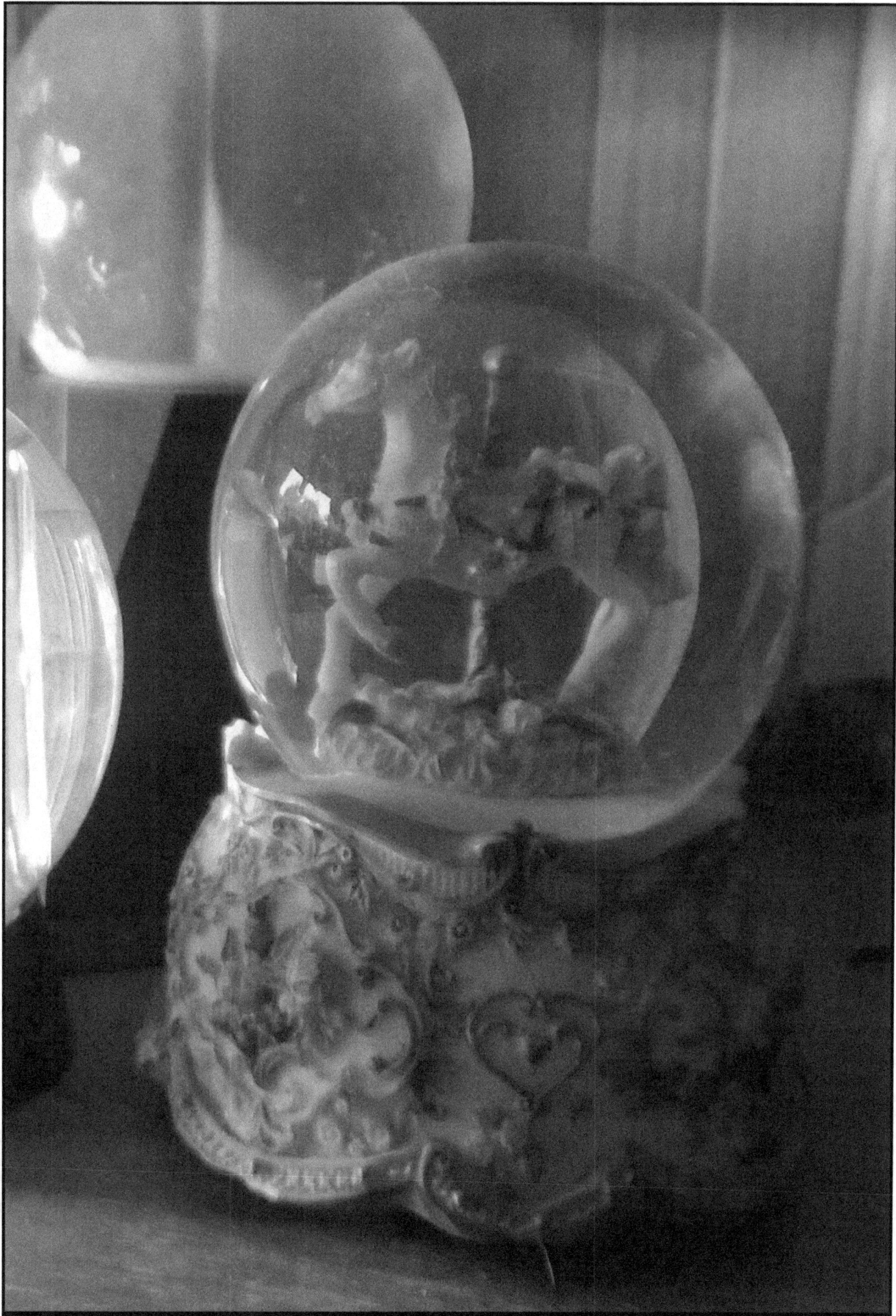

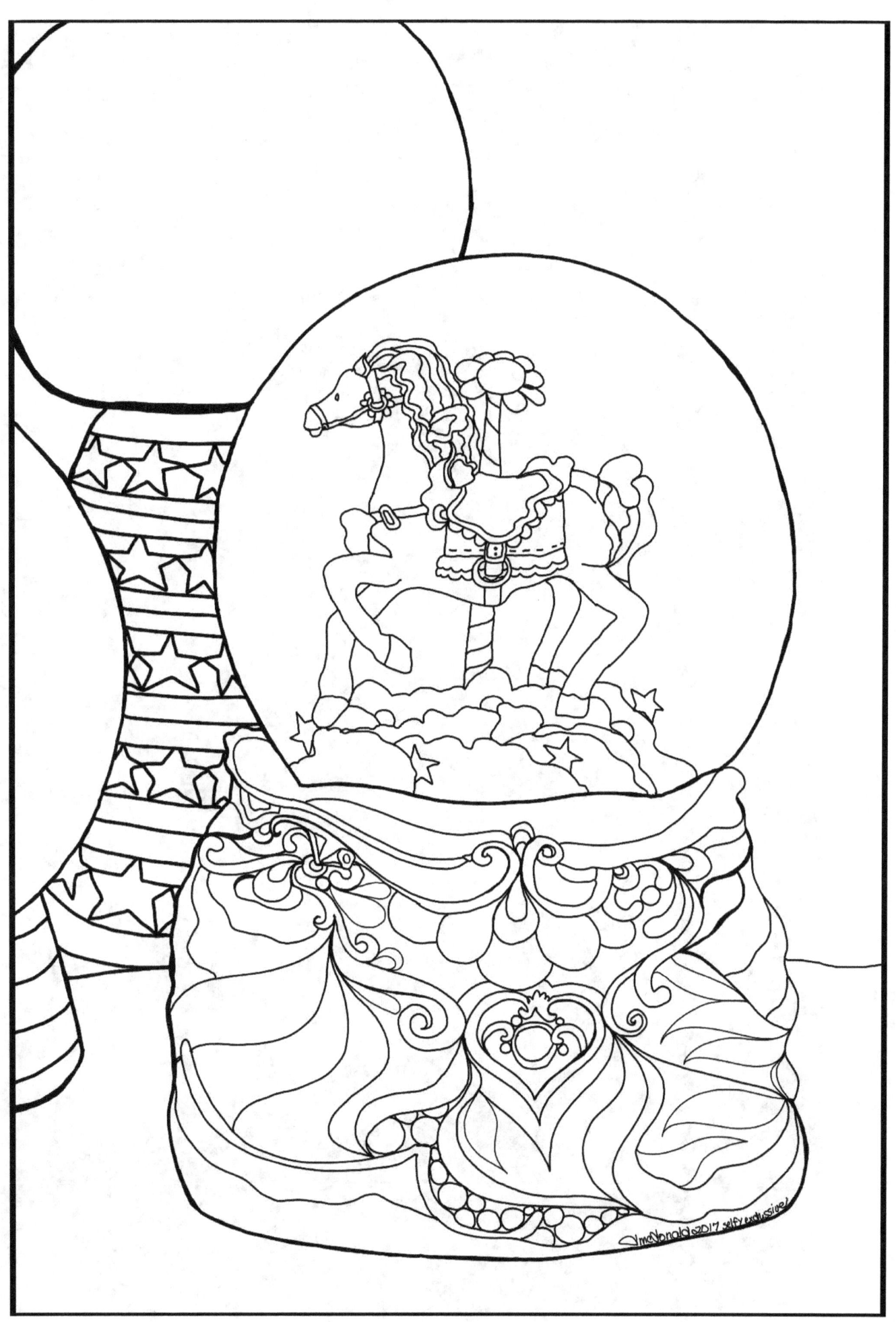

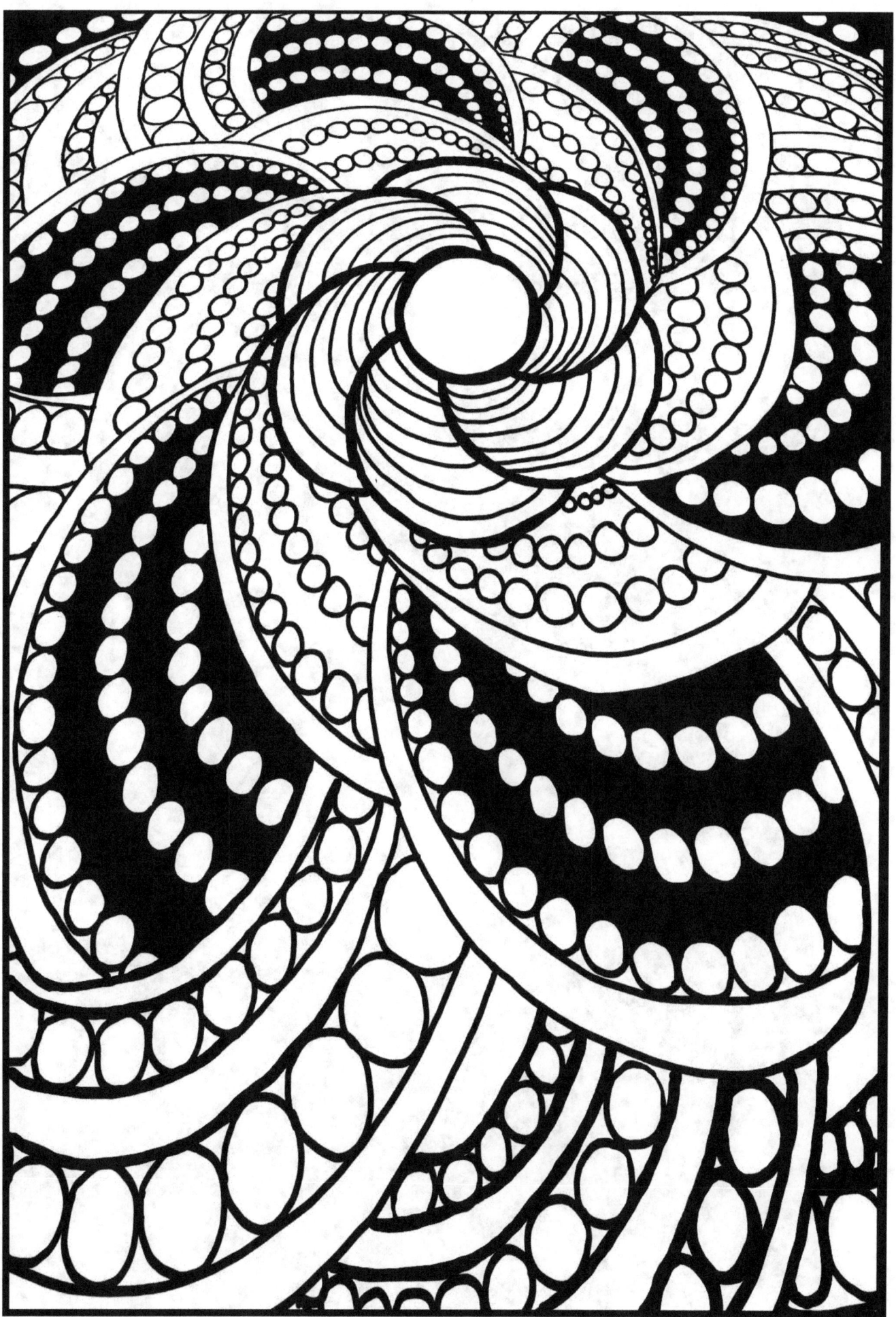

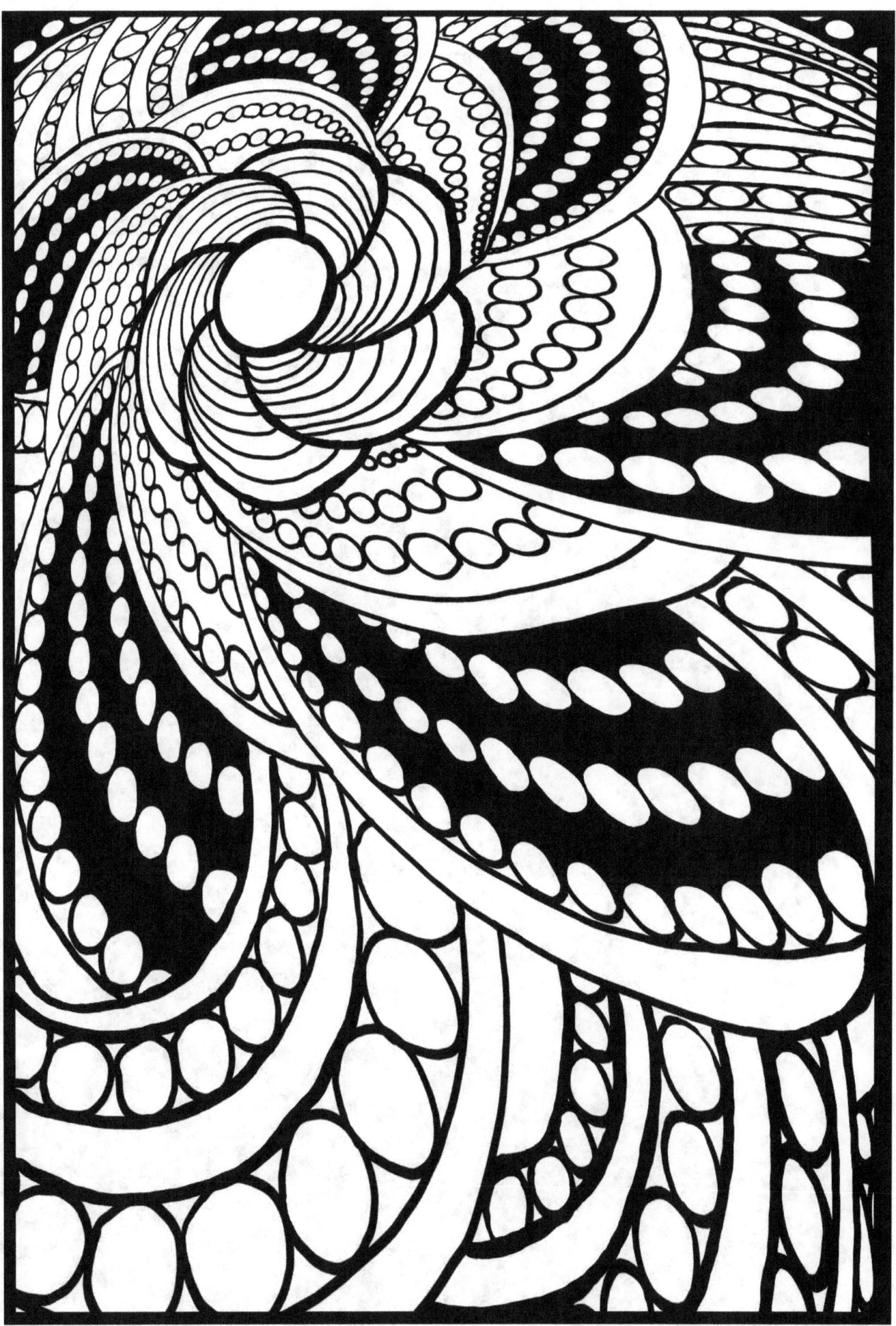

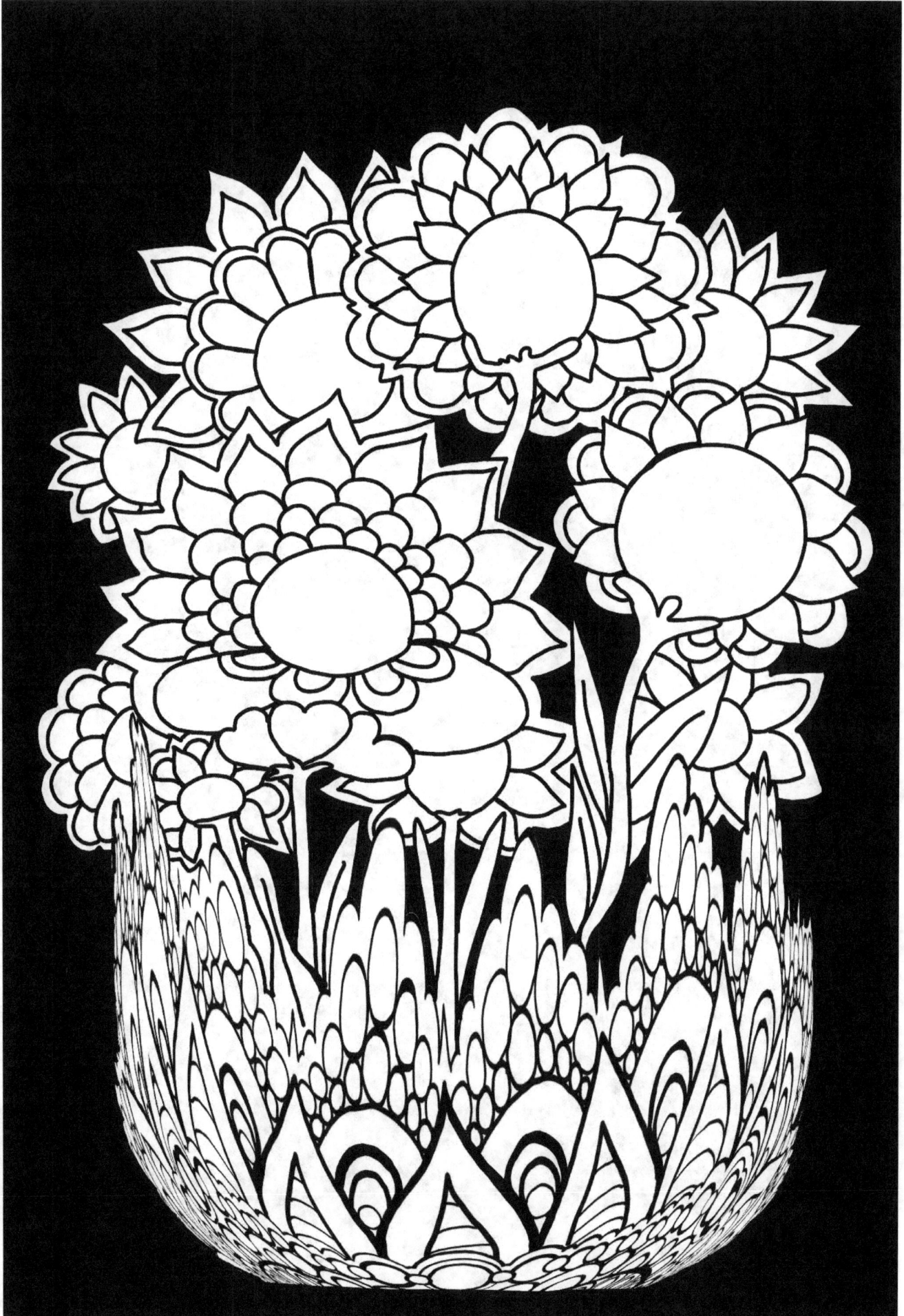

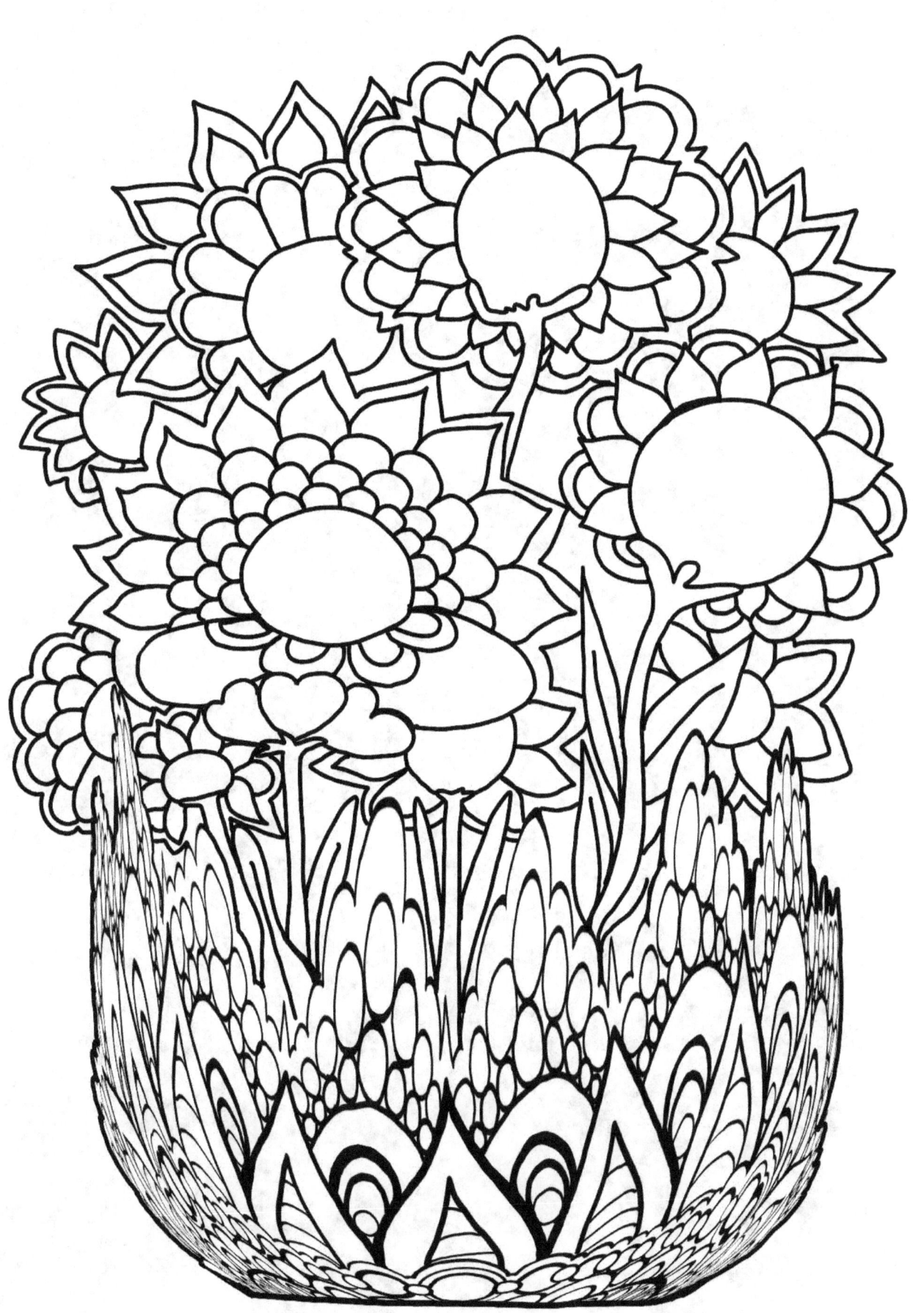

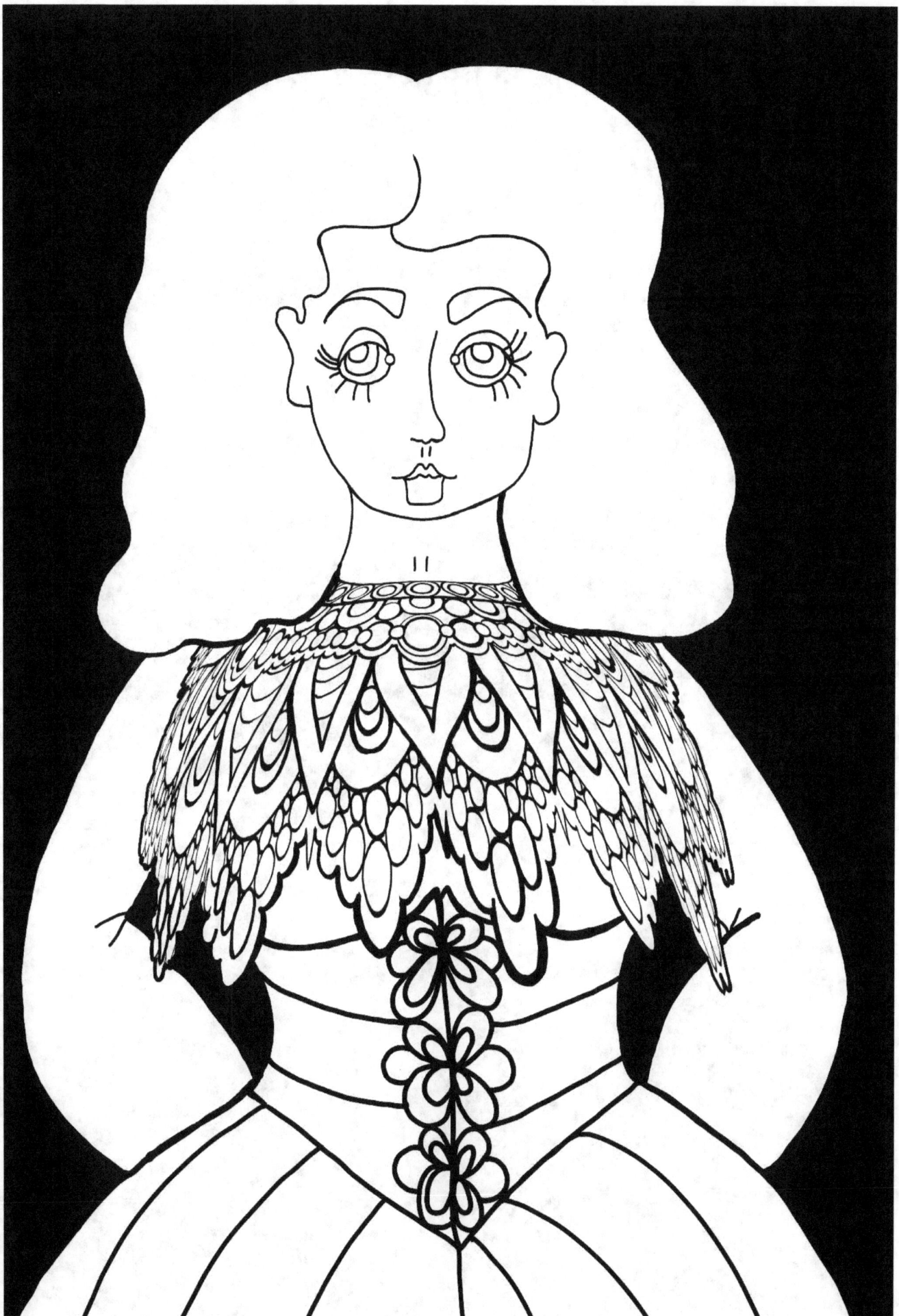

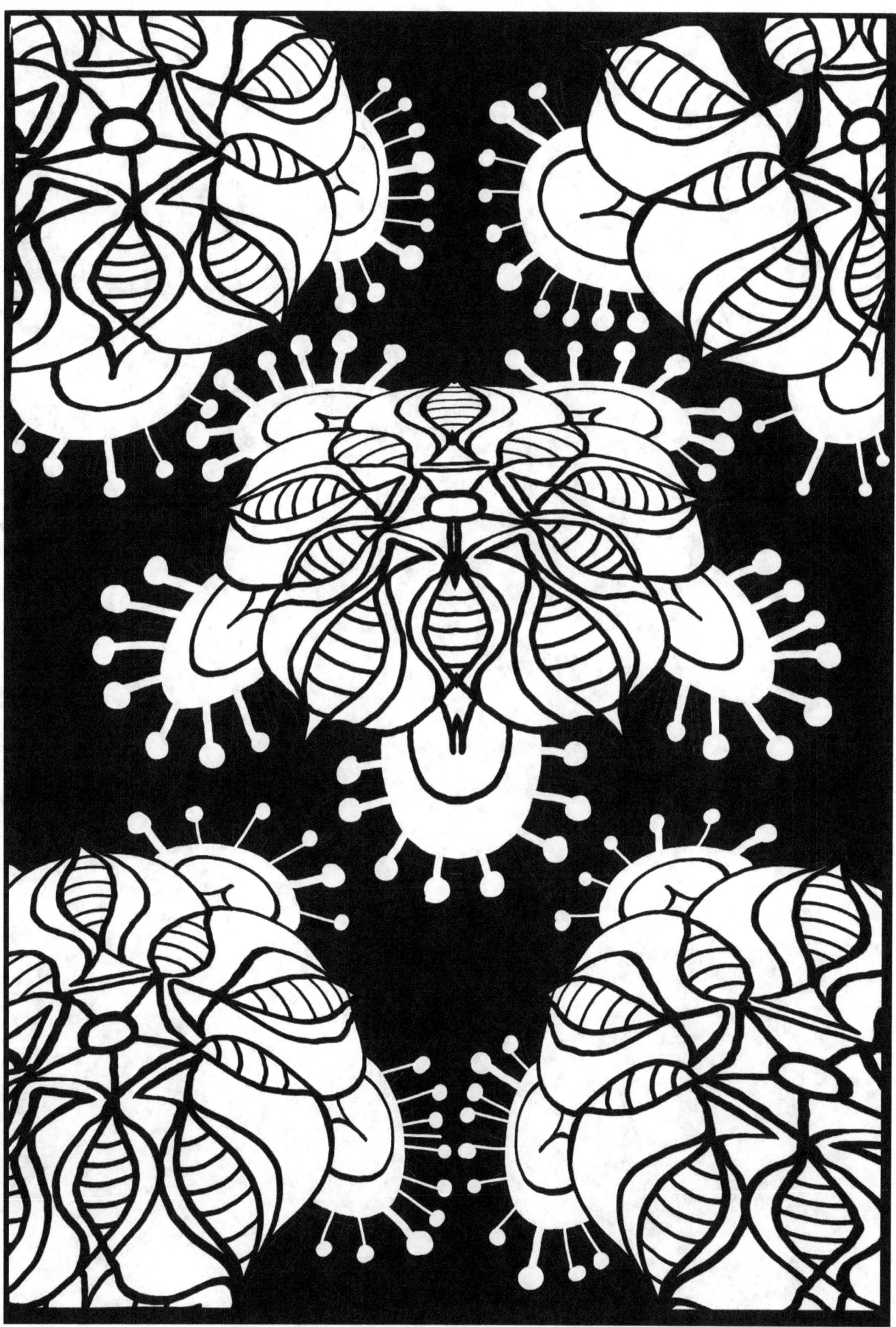

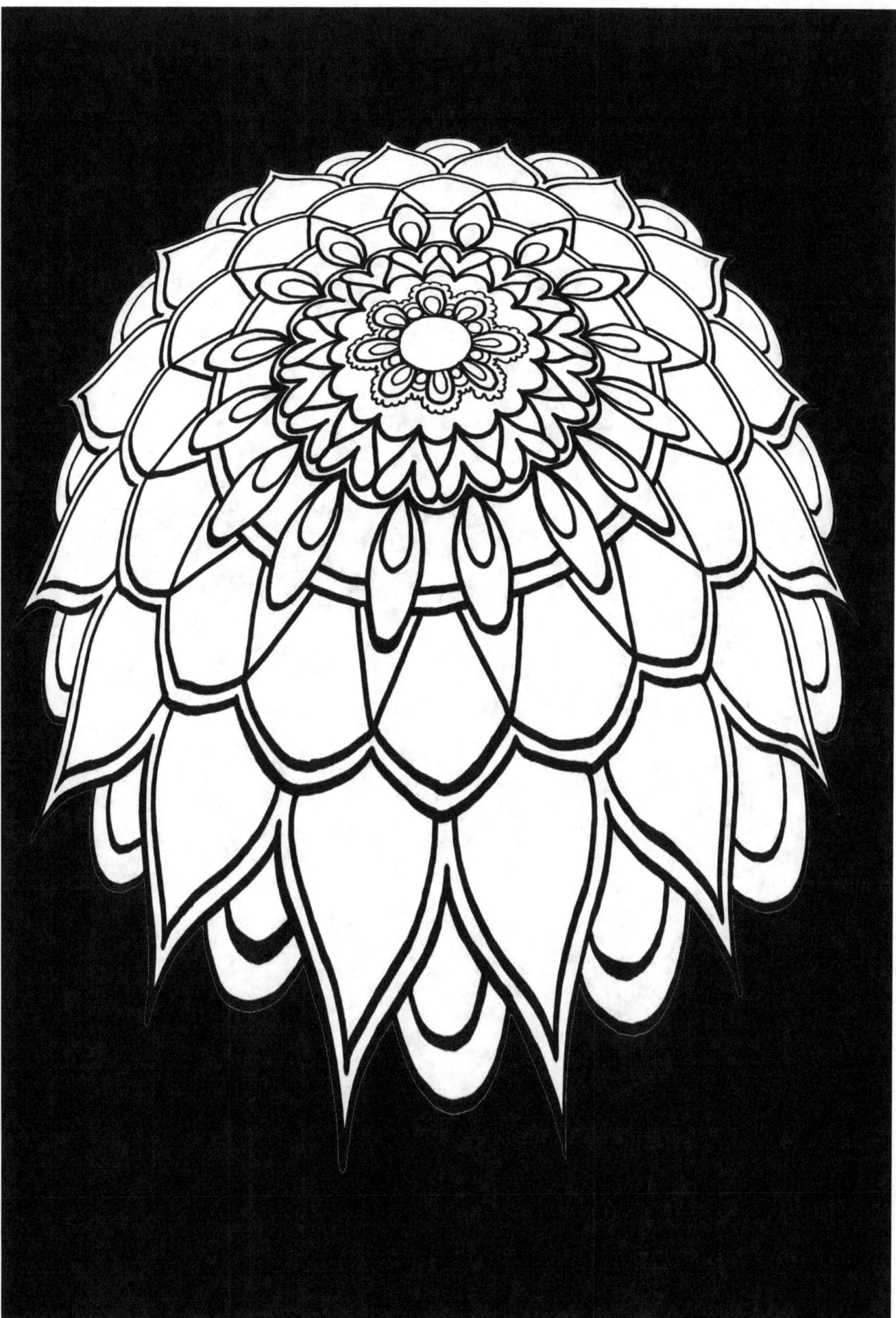

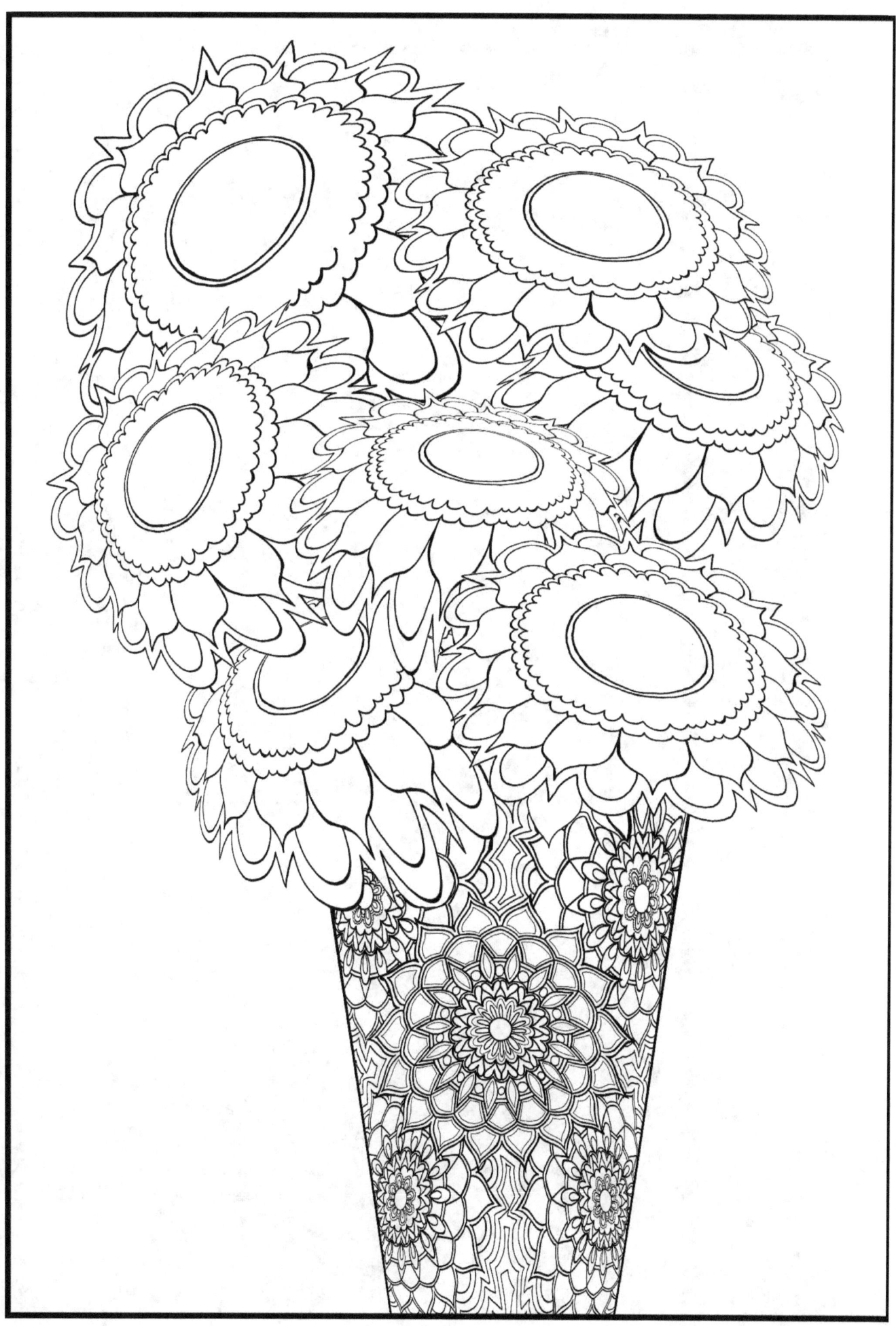

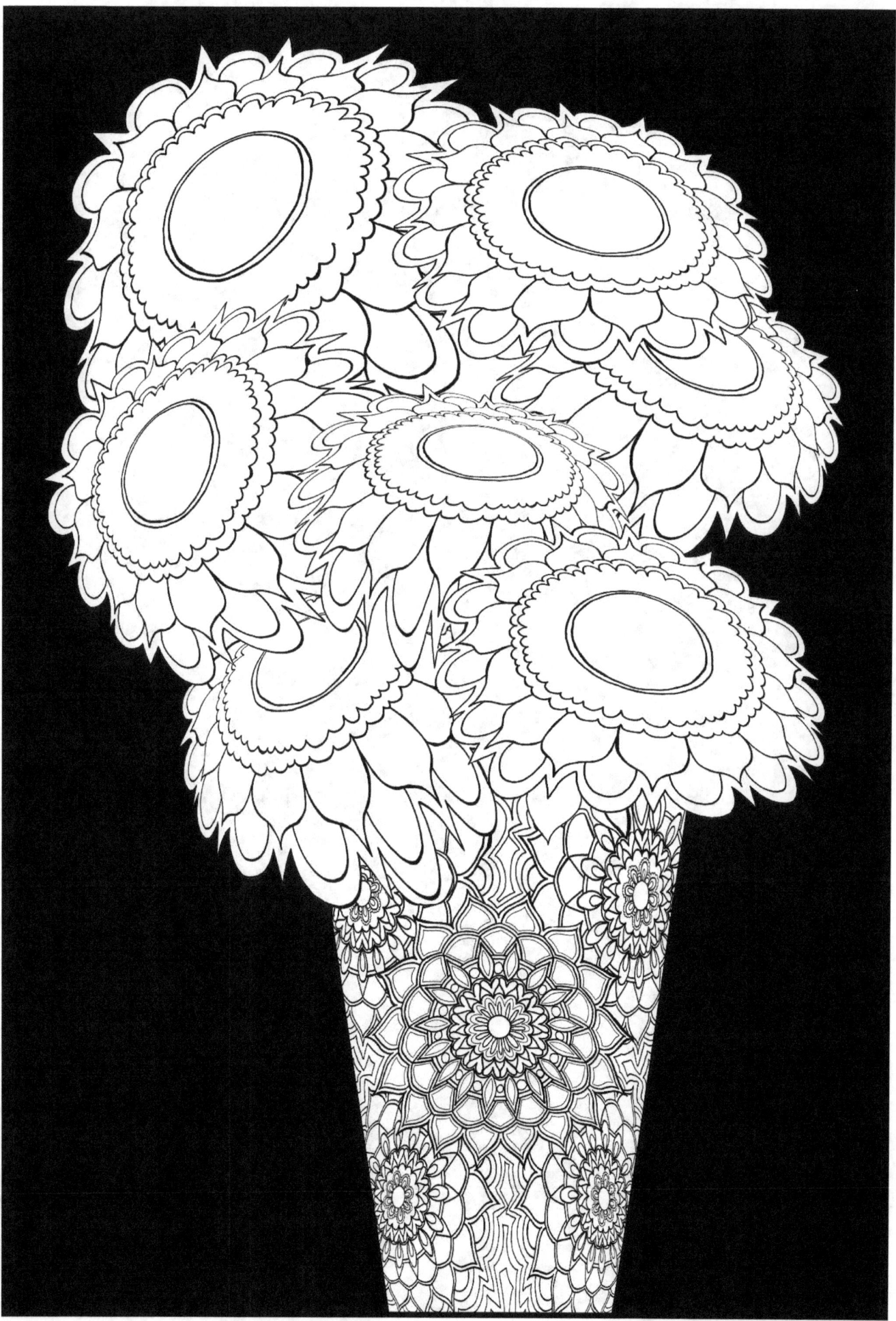

Happy Harvest Time

Harvest Time

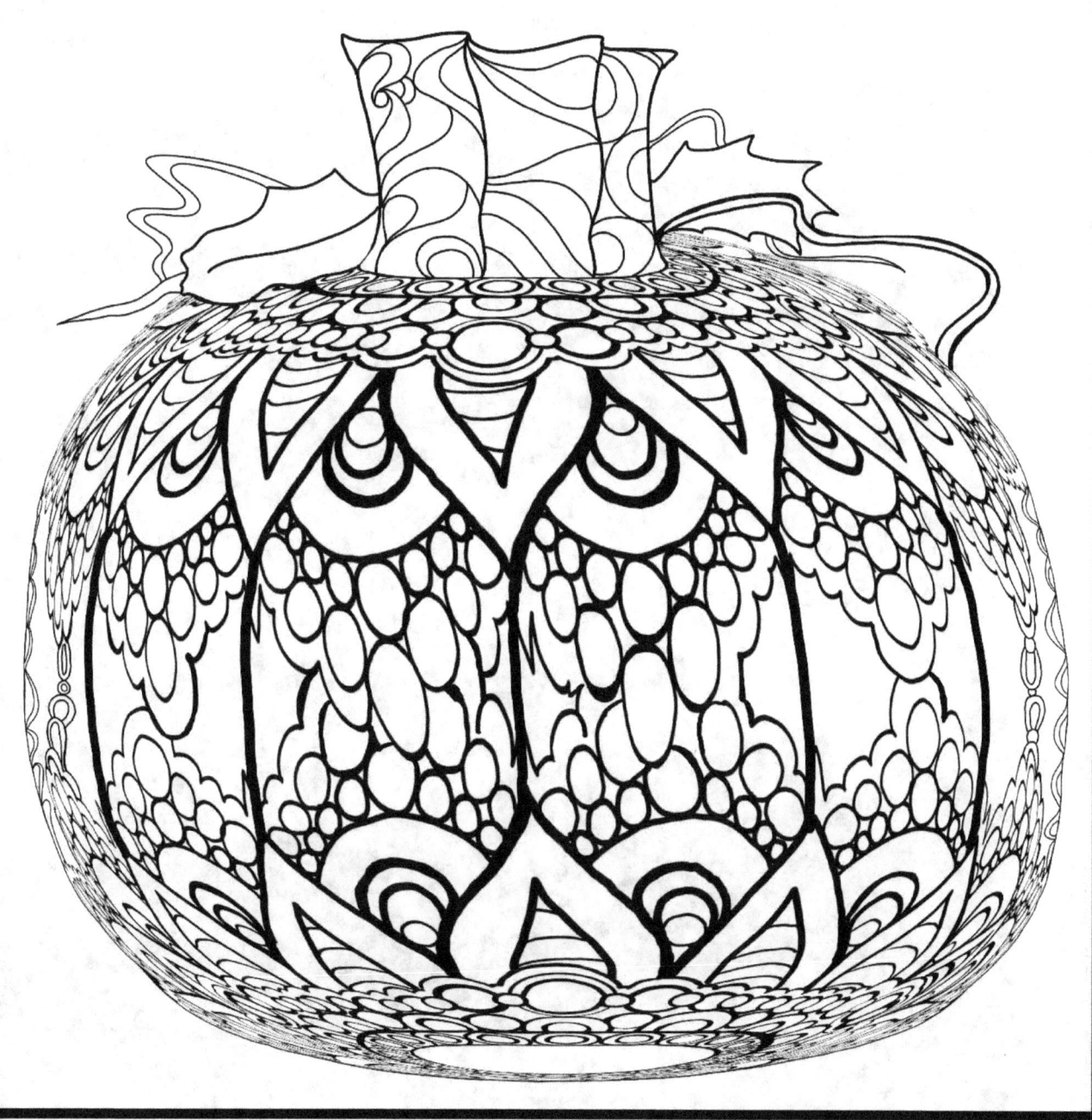

Harvest Time

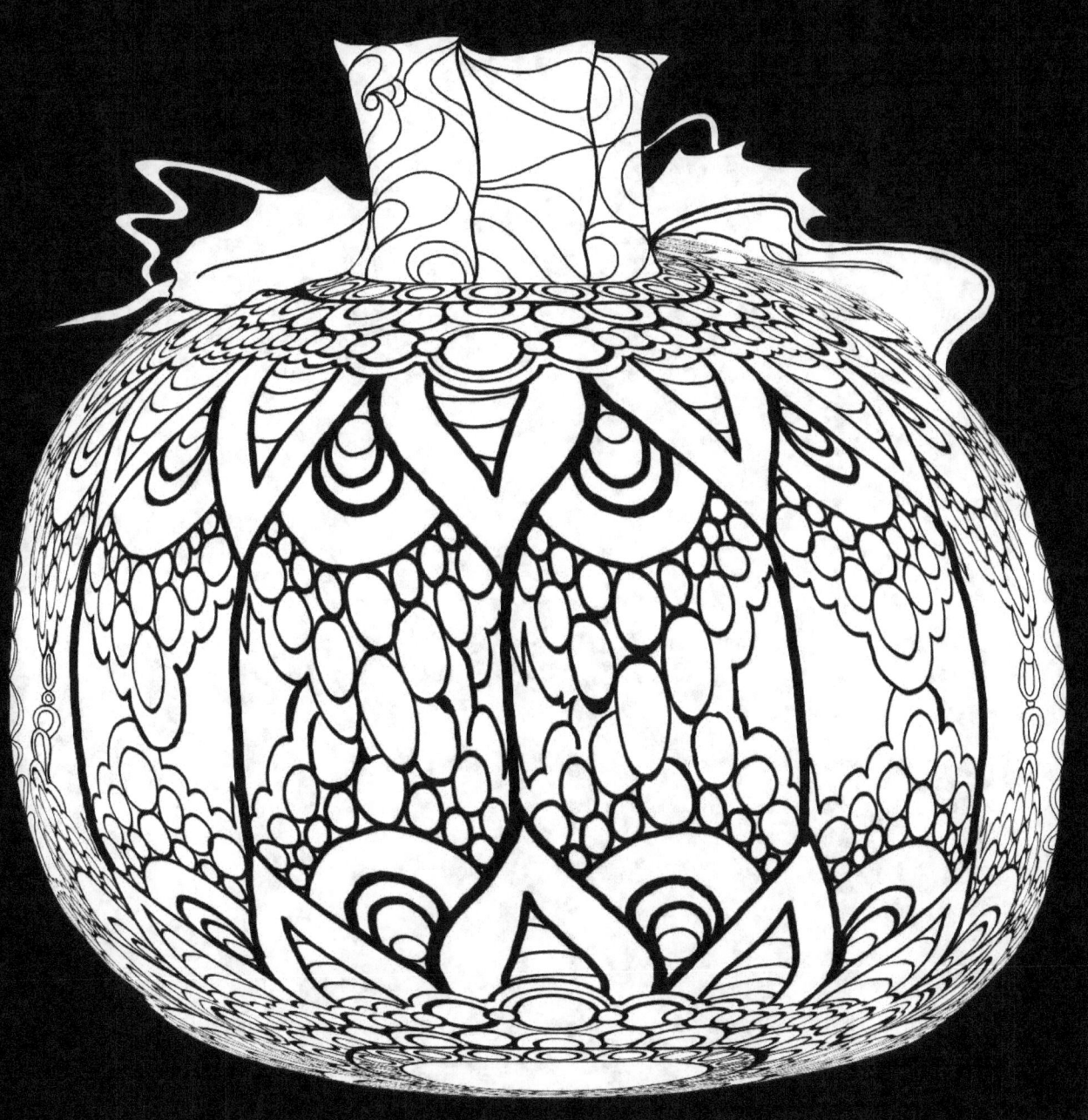

Harvest Time

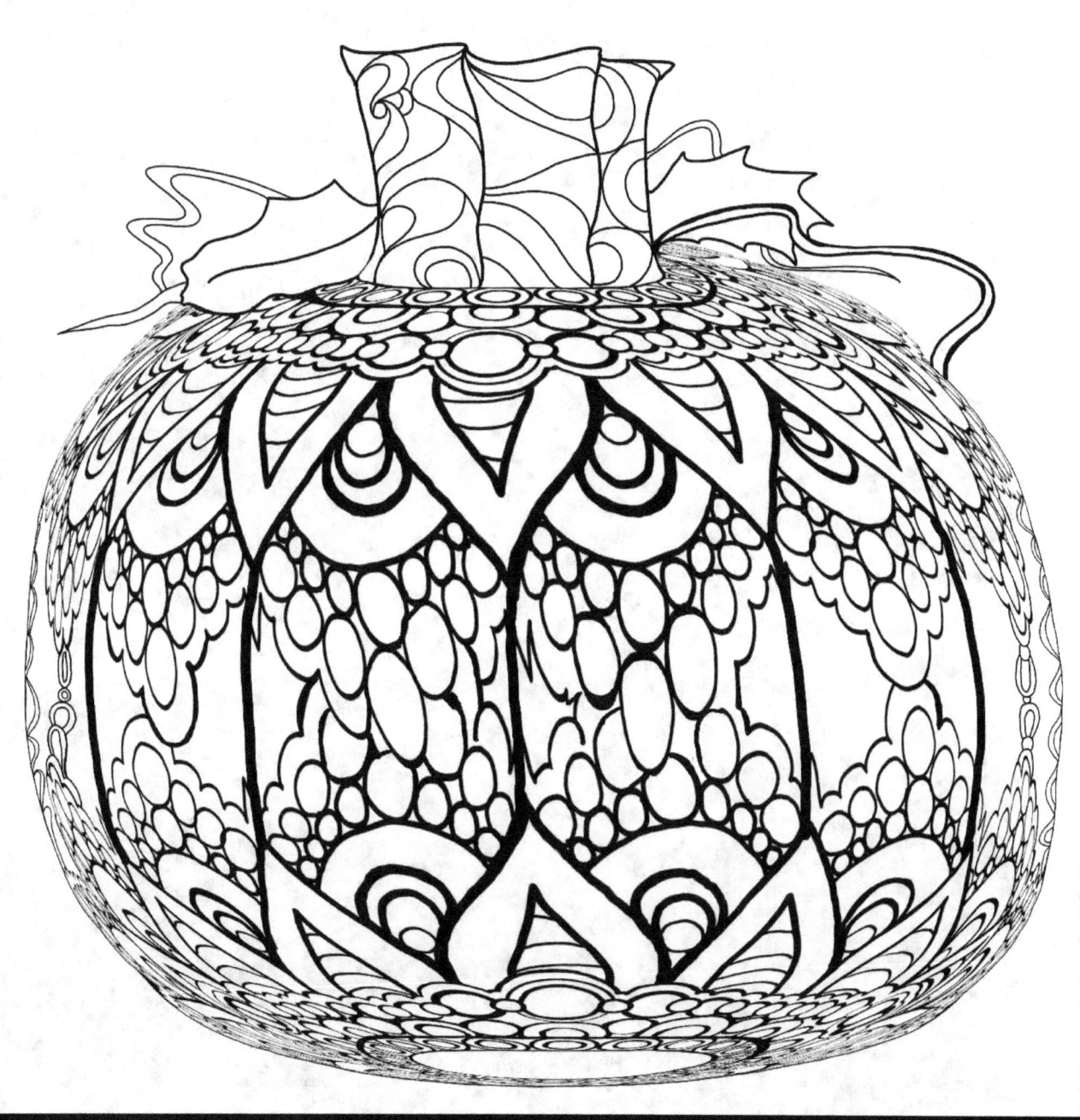

Harvest Time

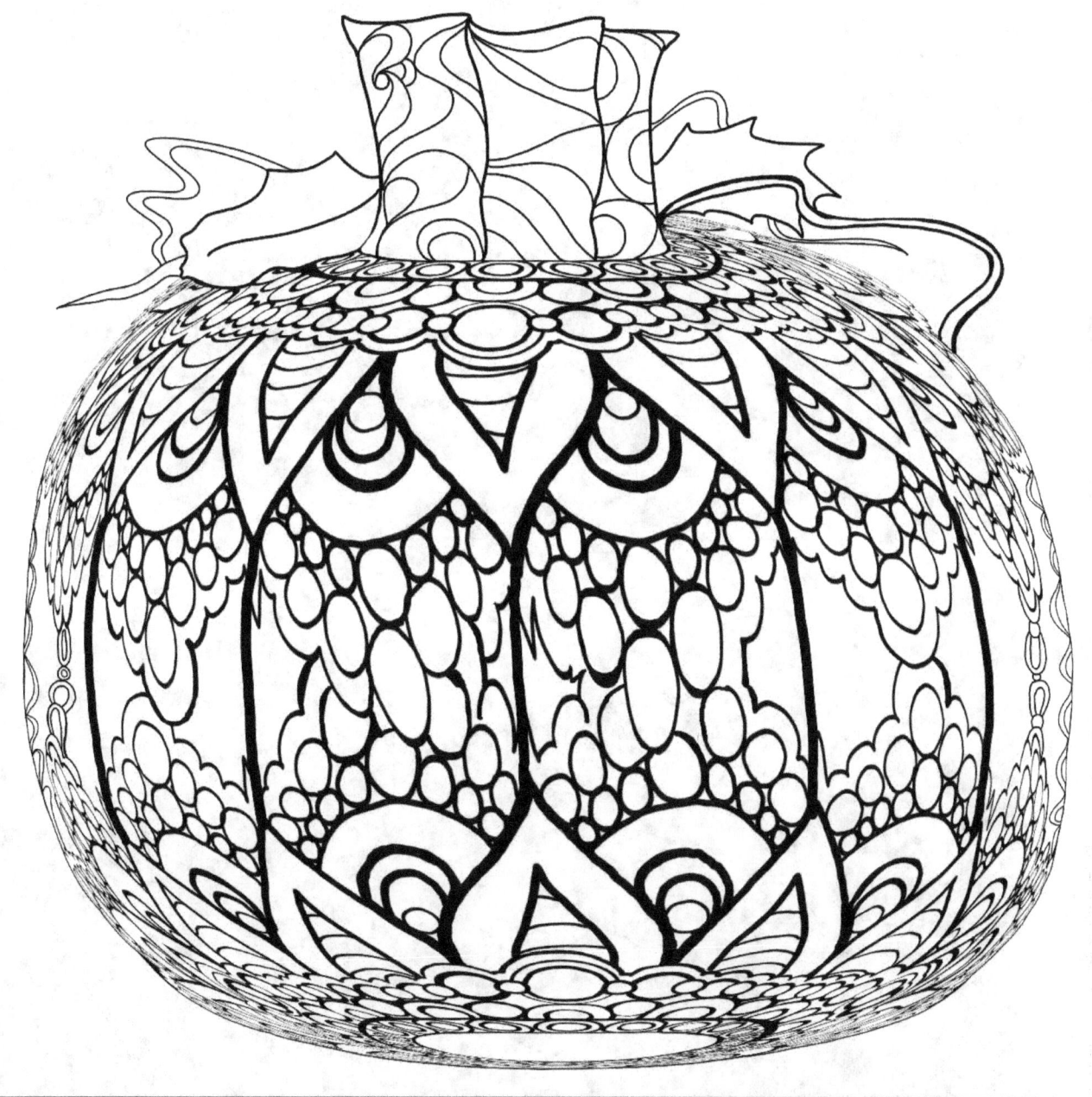

Harvest Time

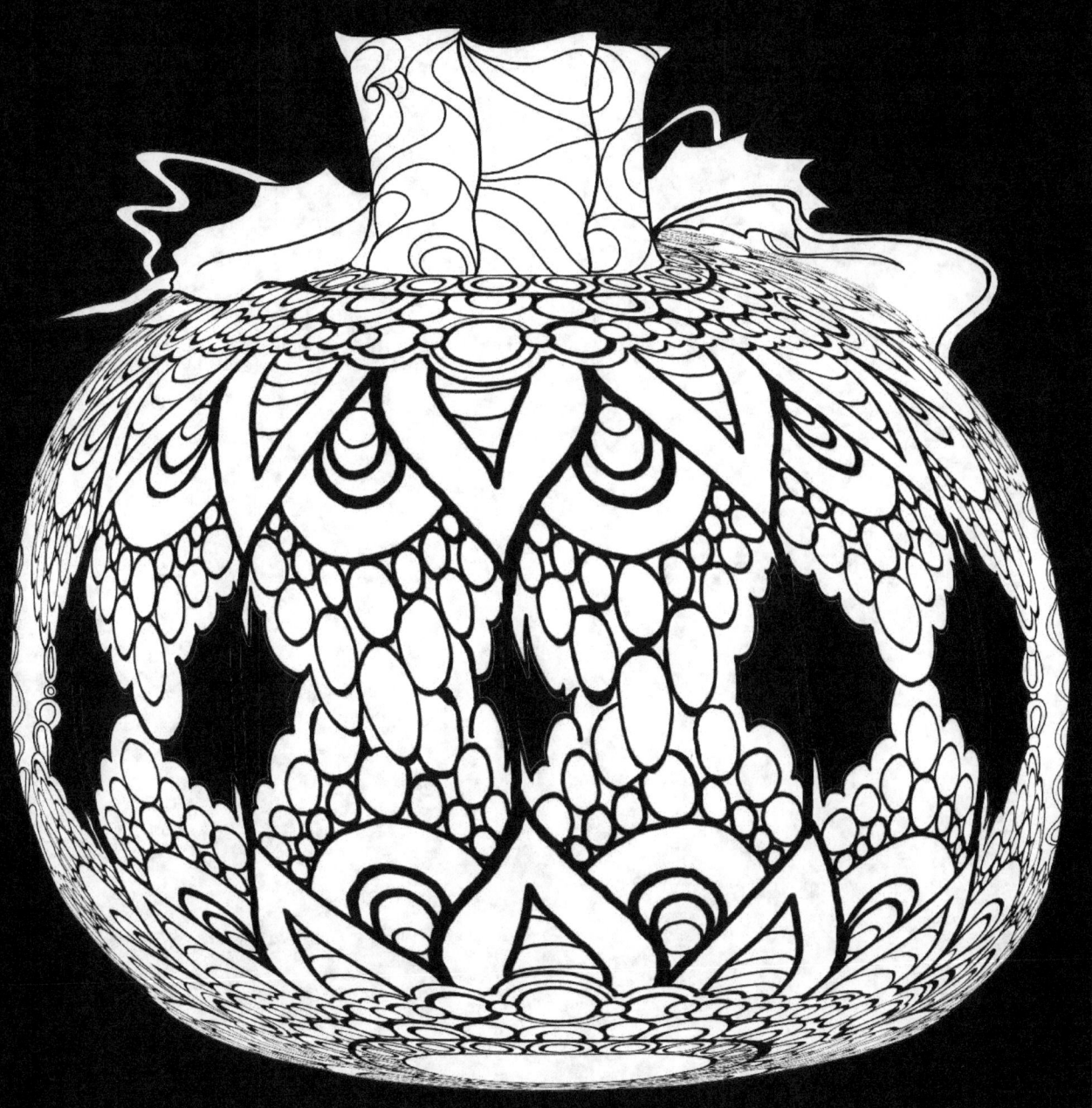

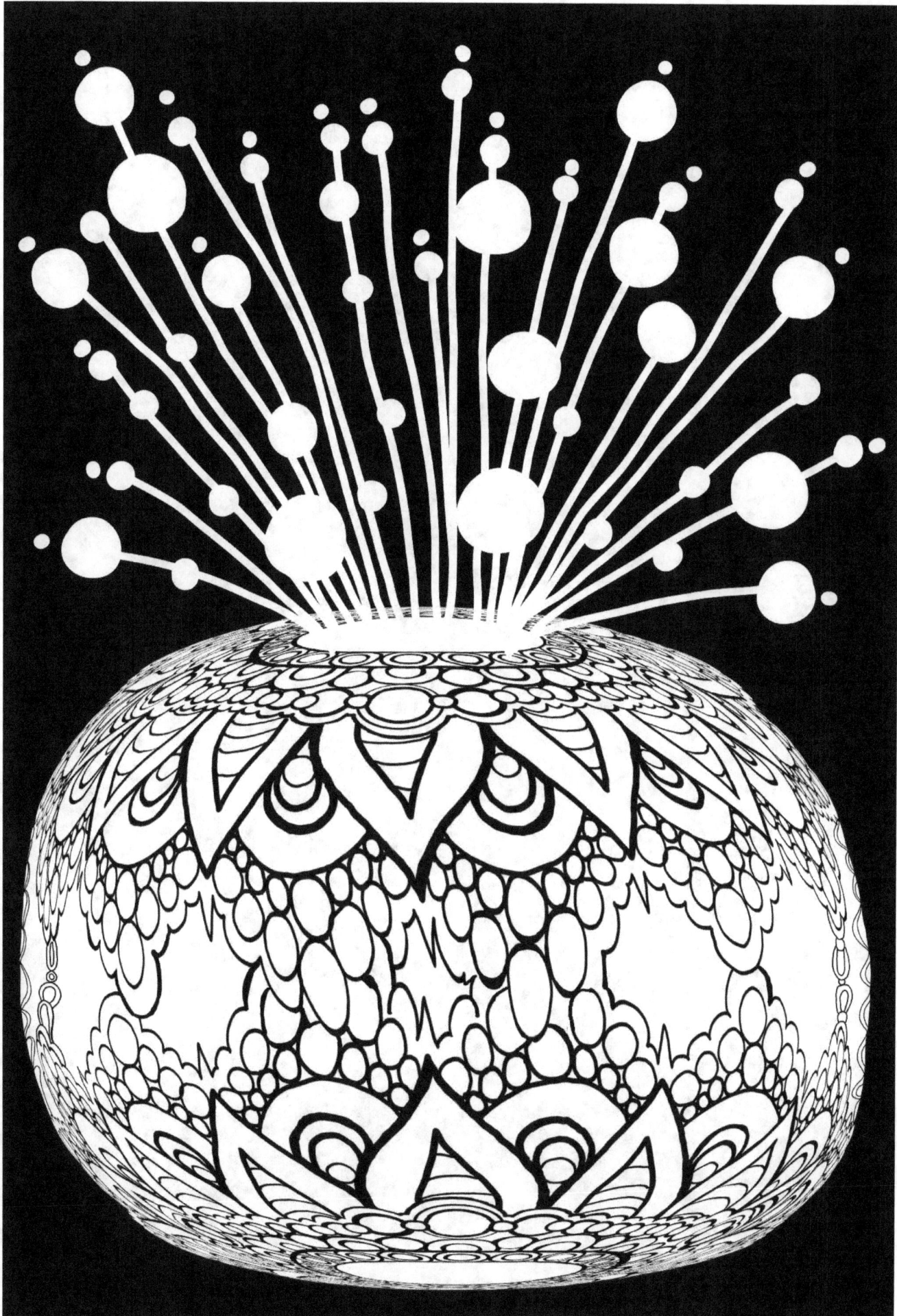

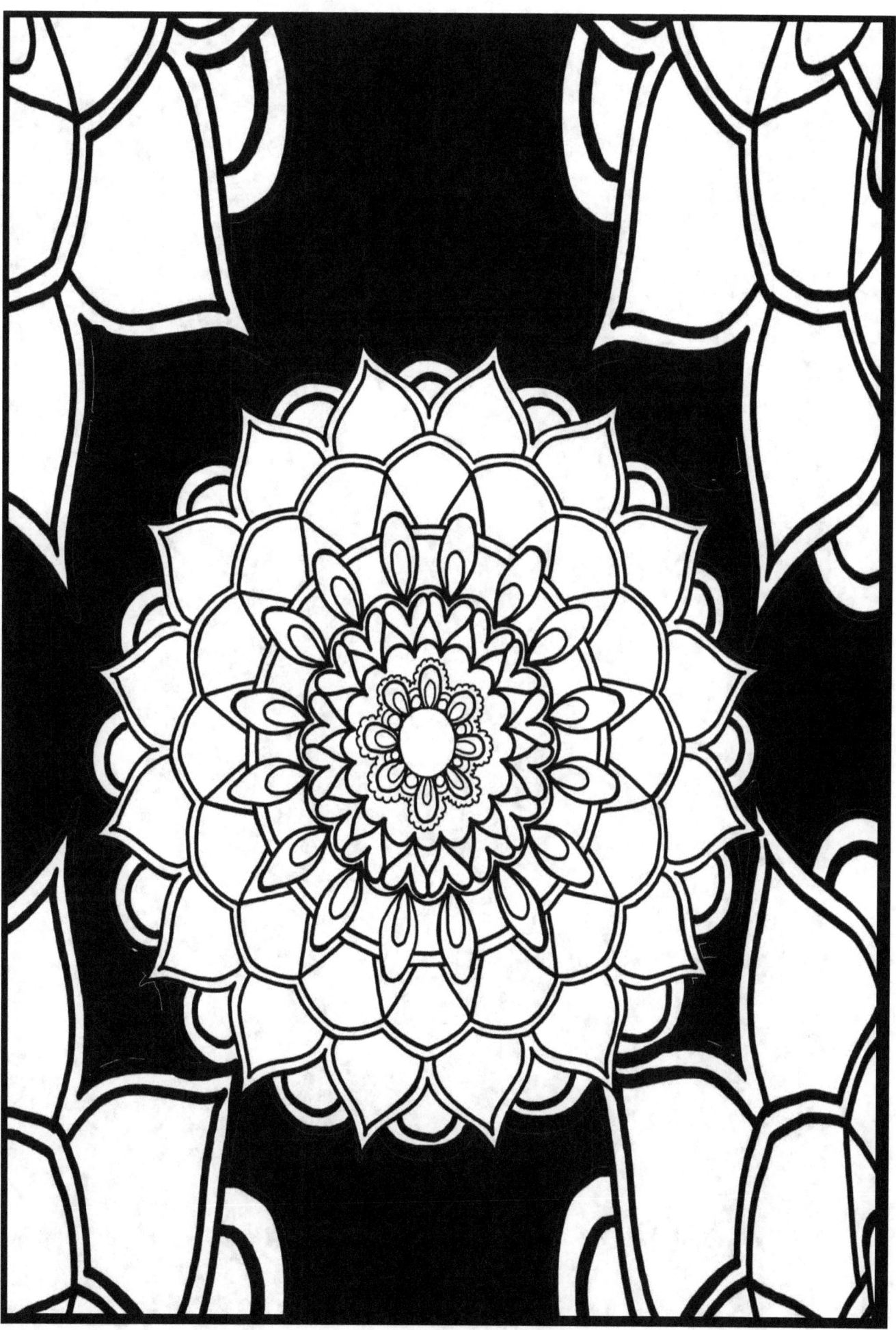

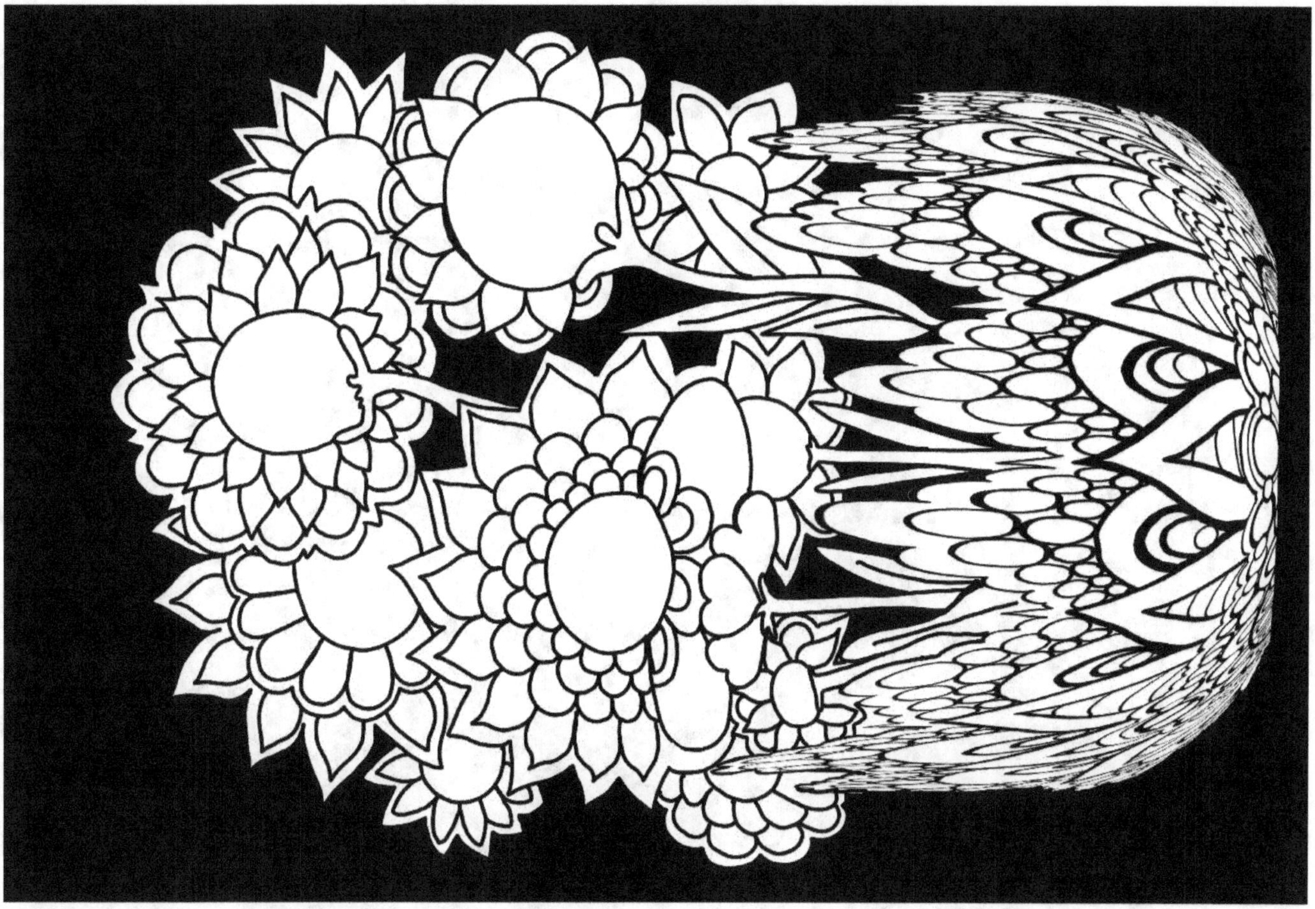

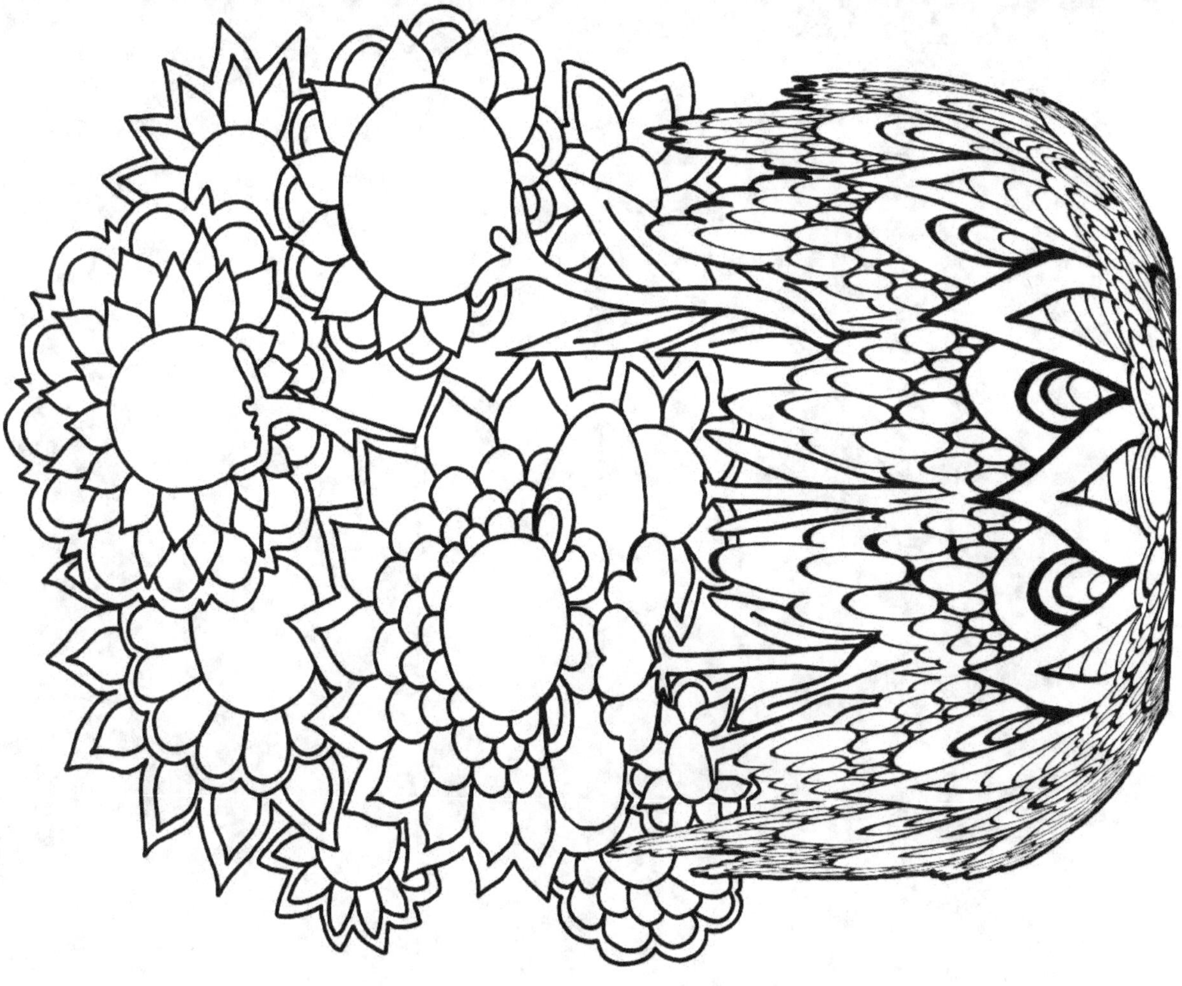

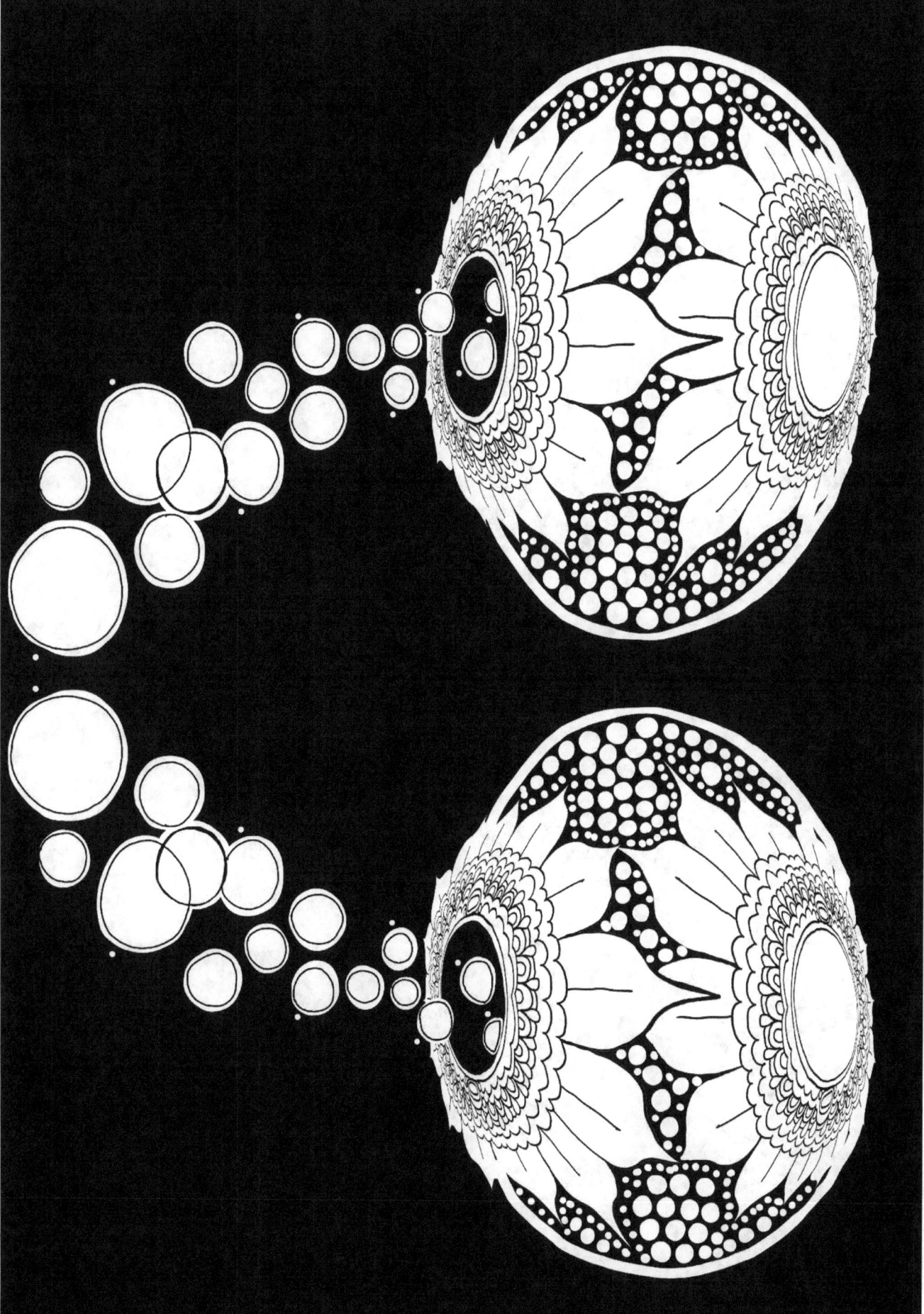

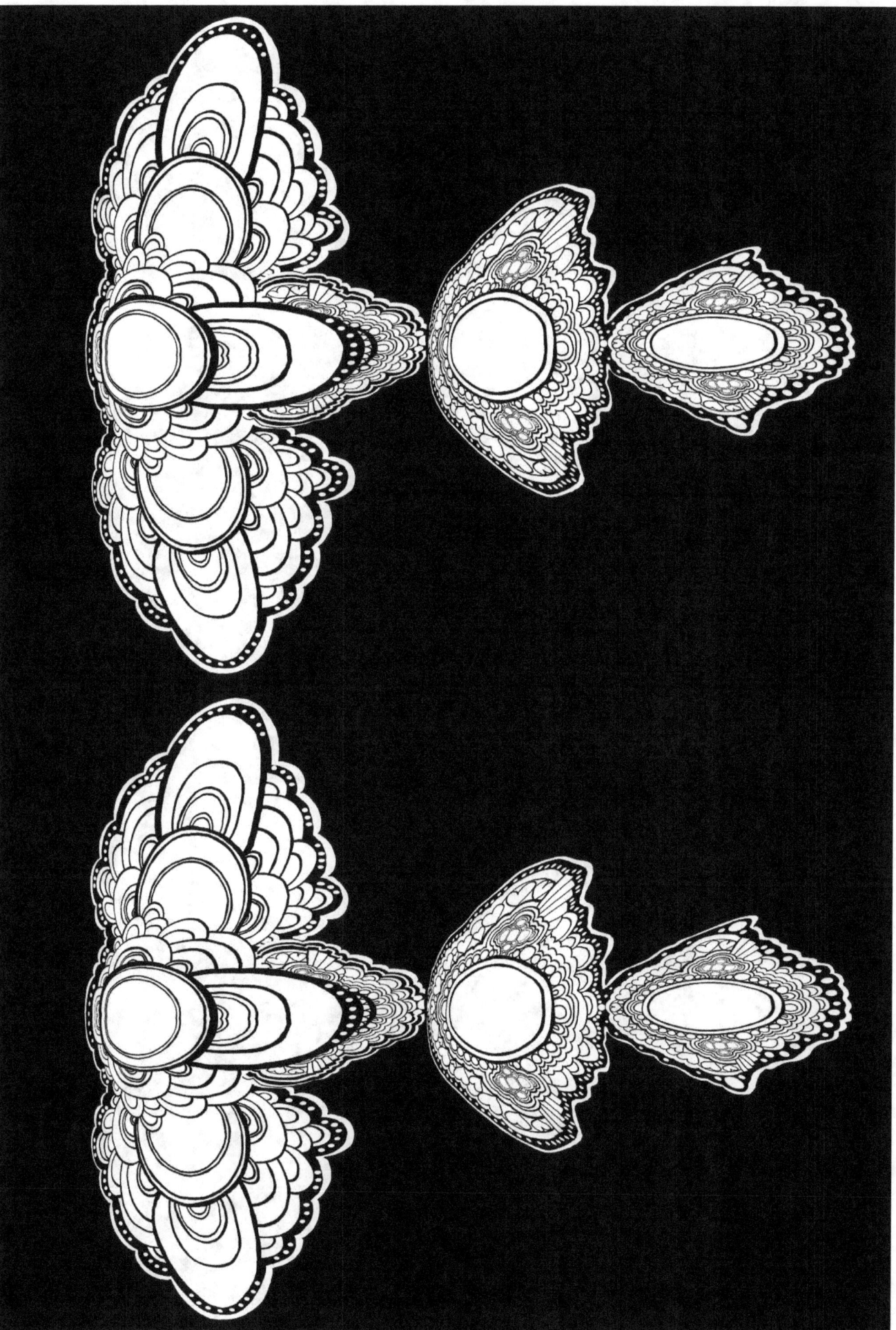

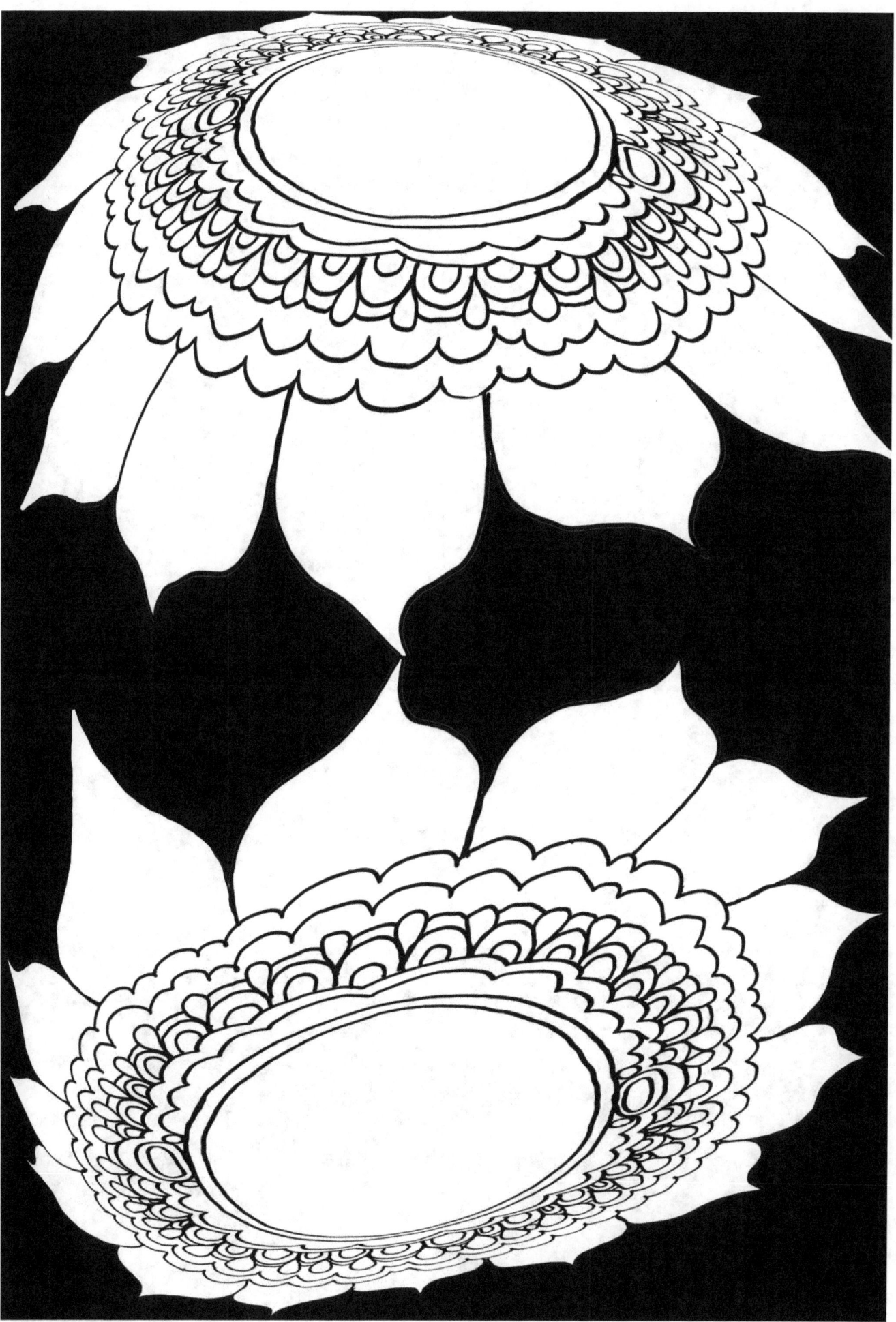

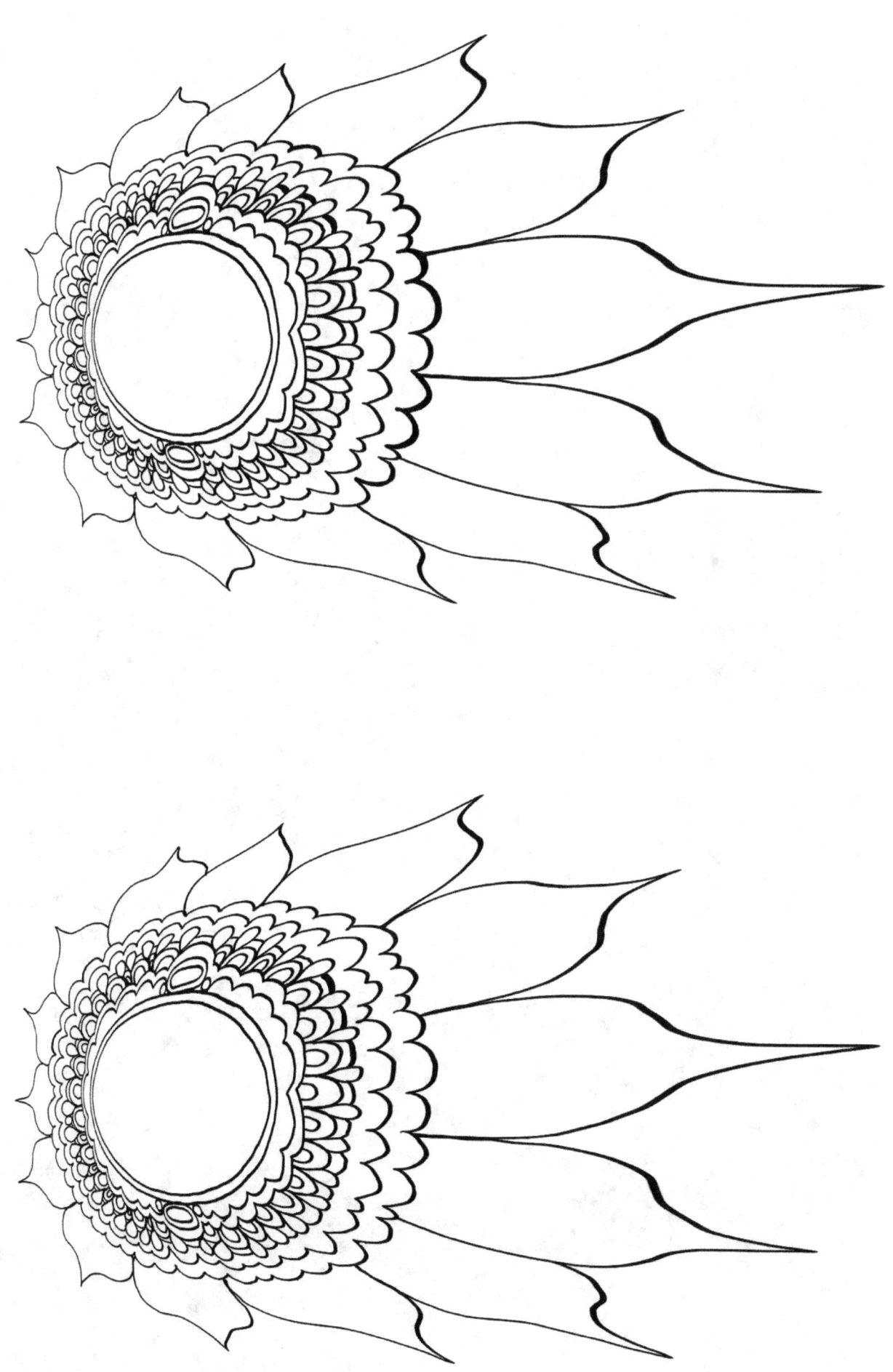

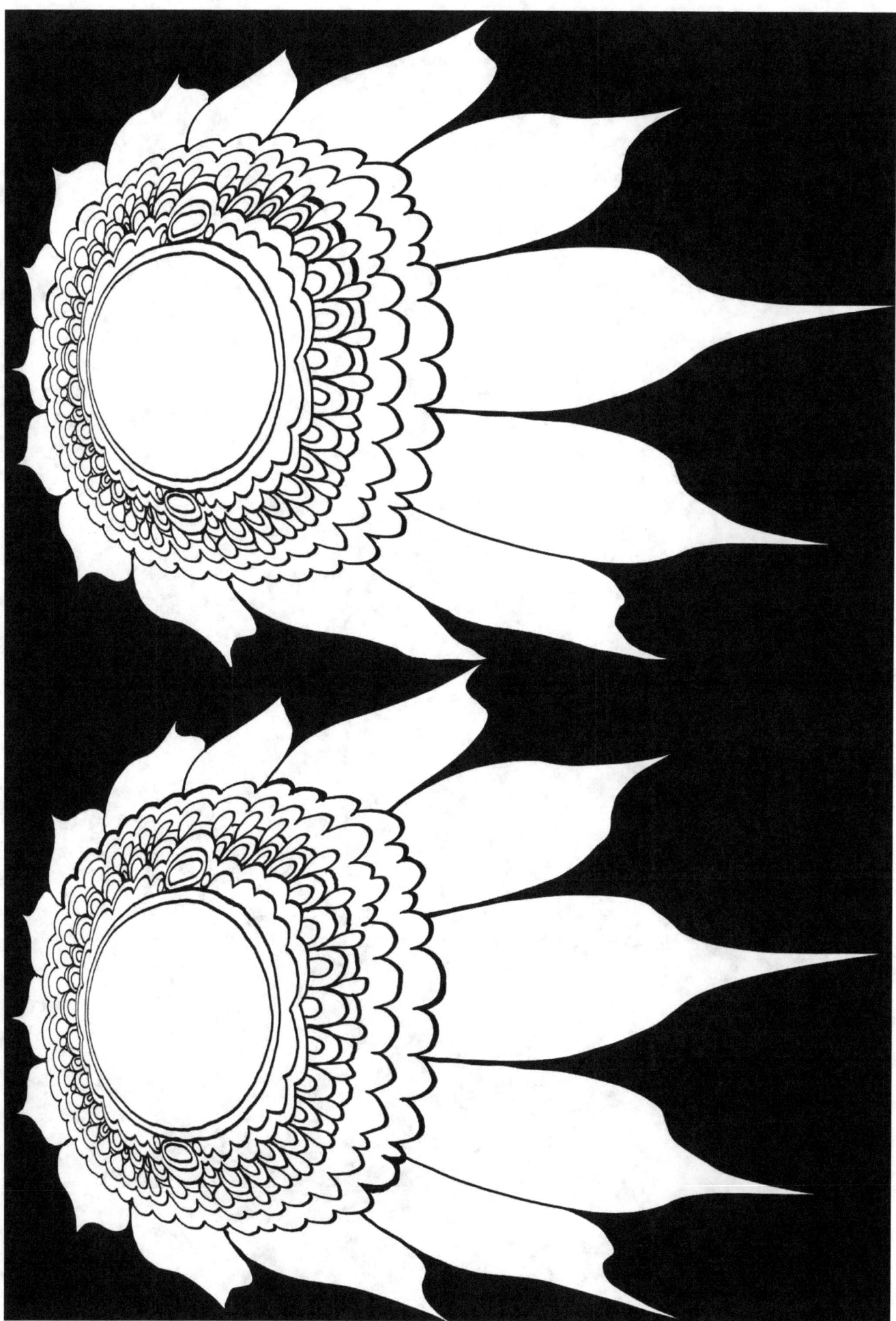

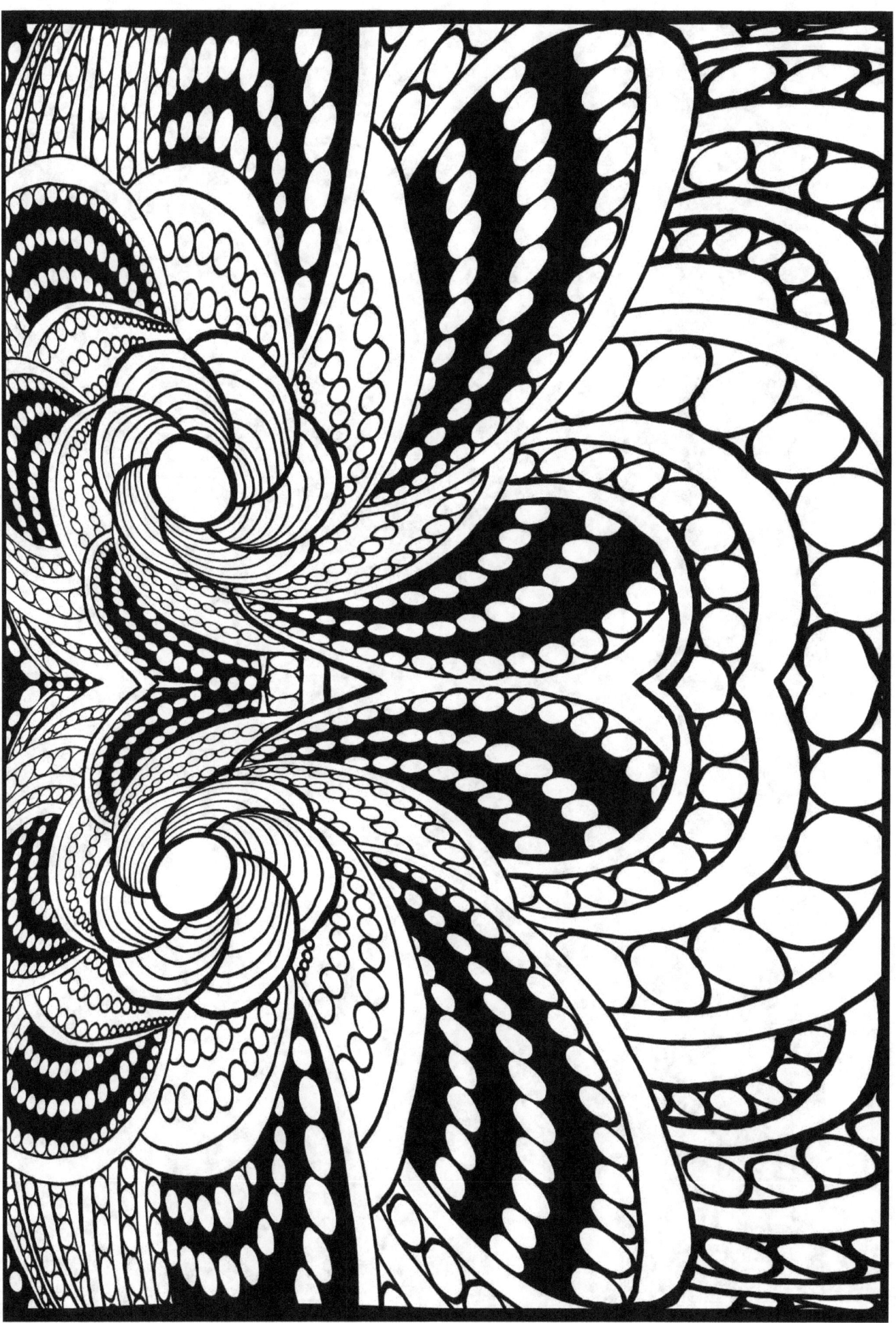

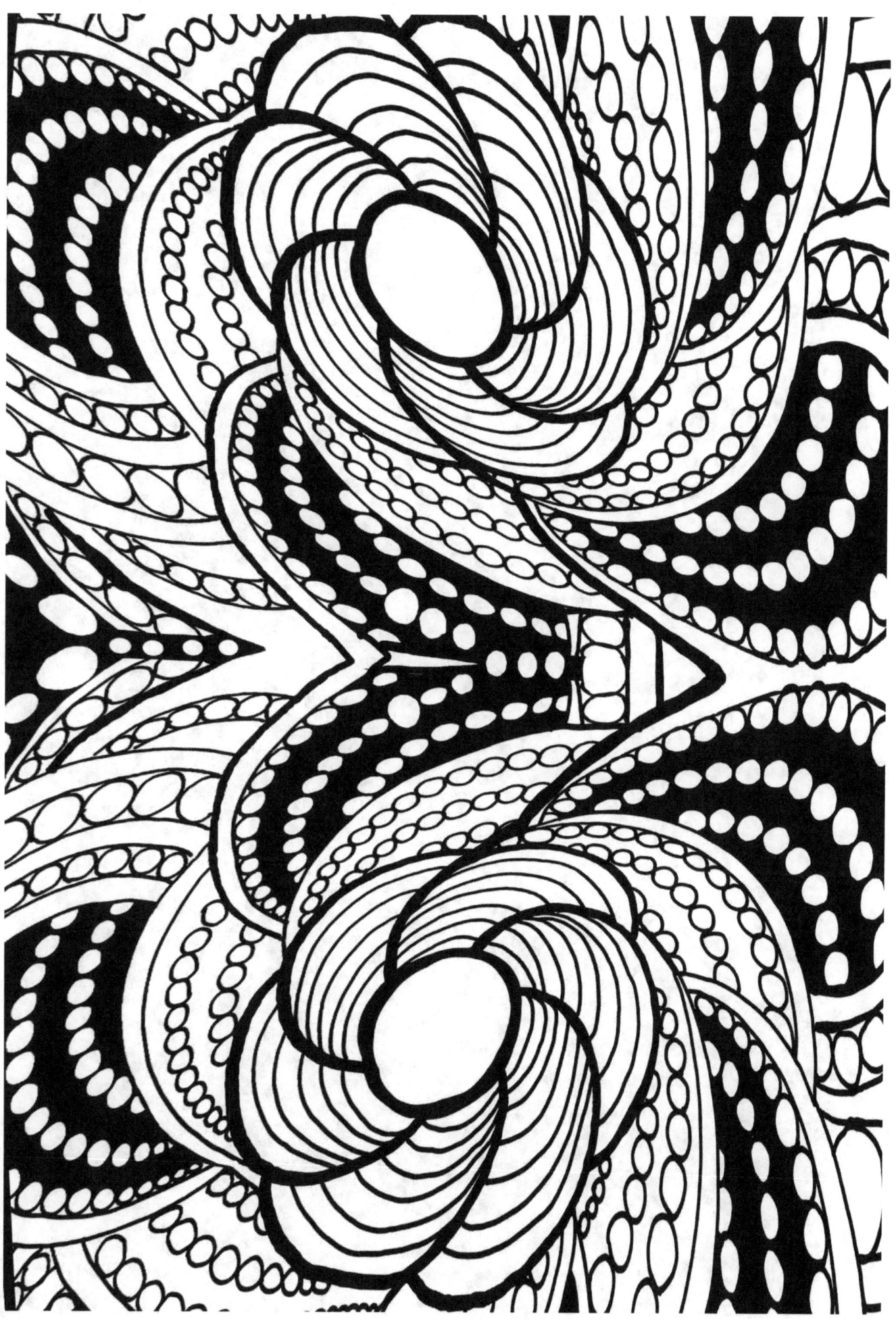

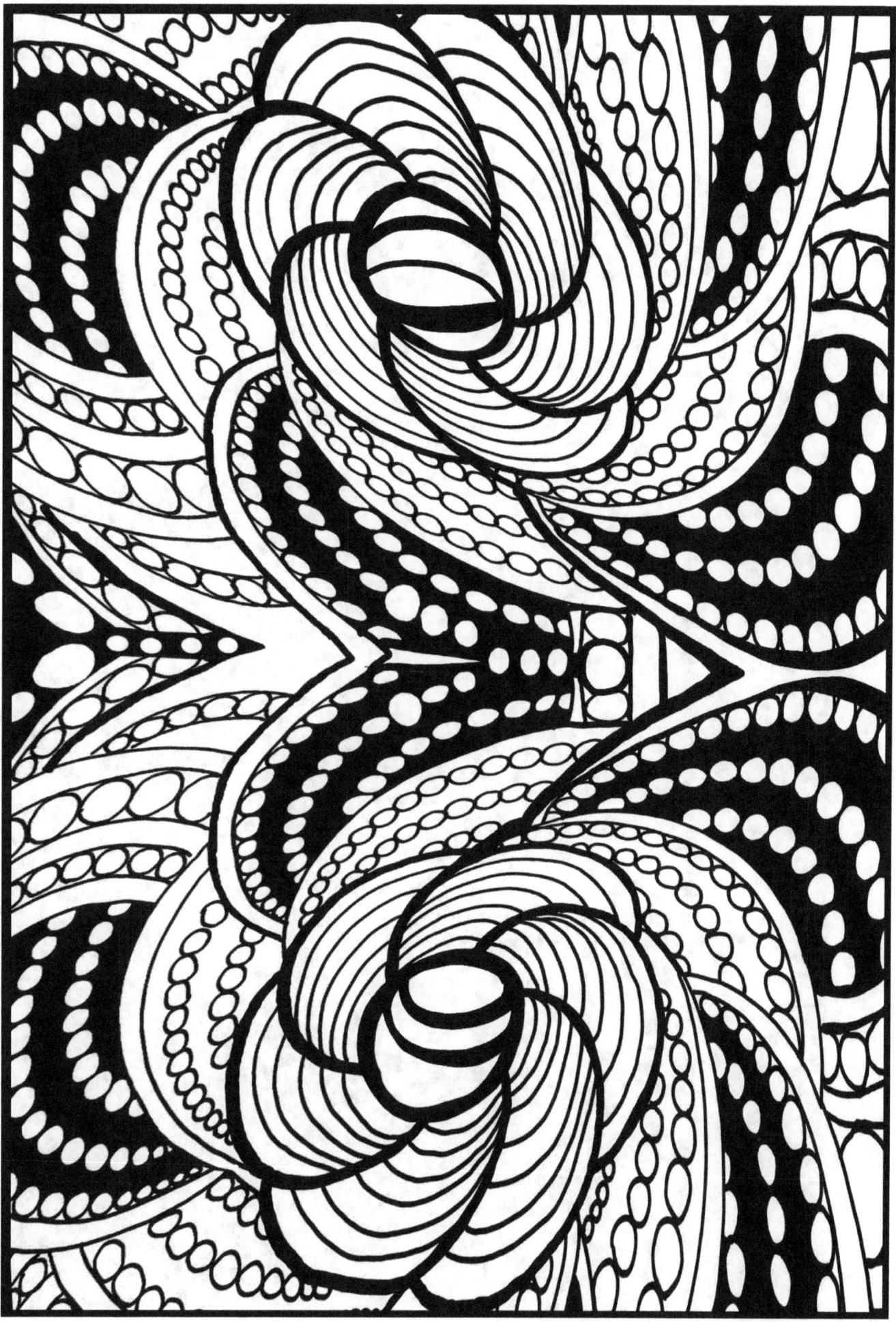

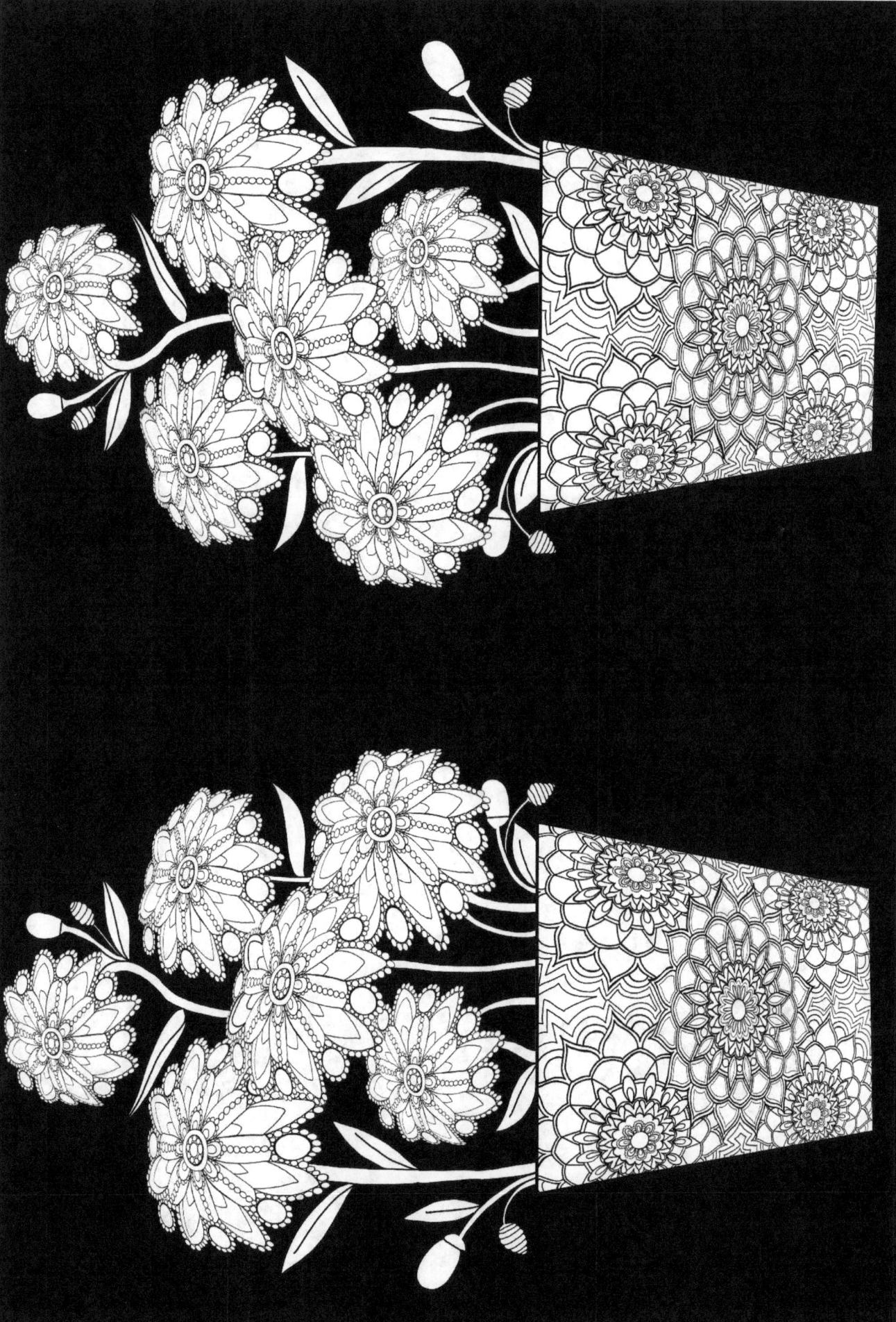

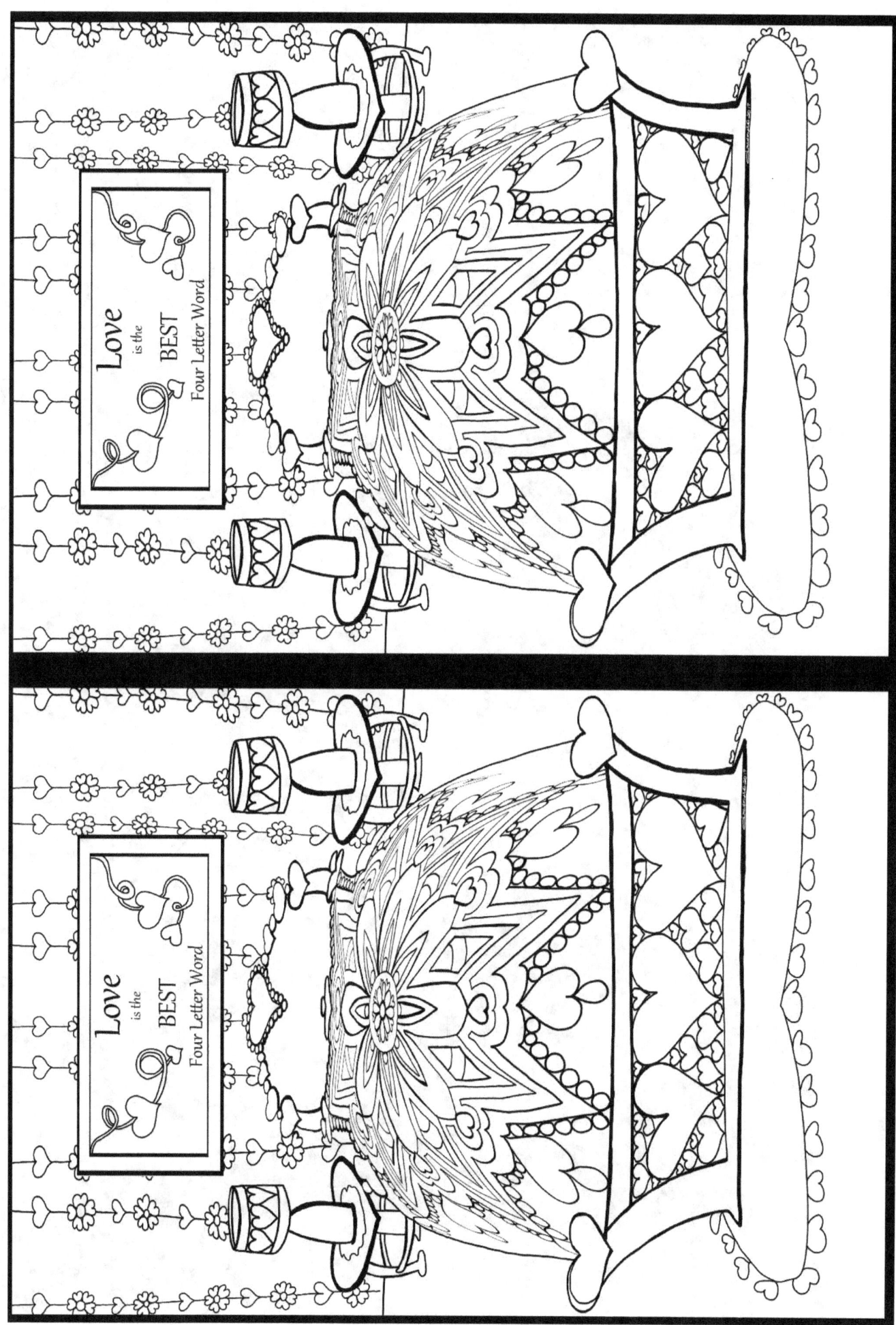

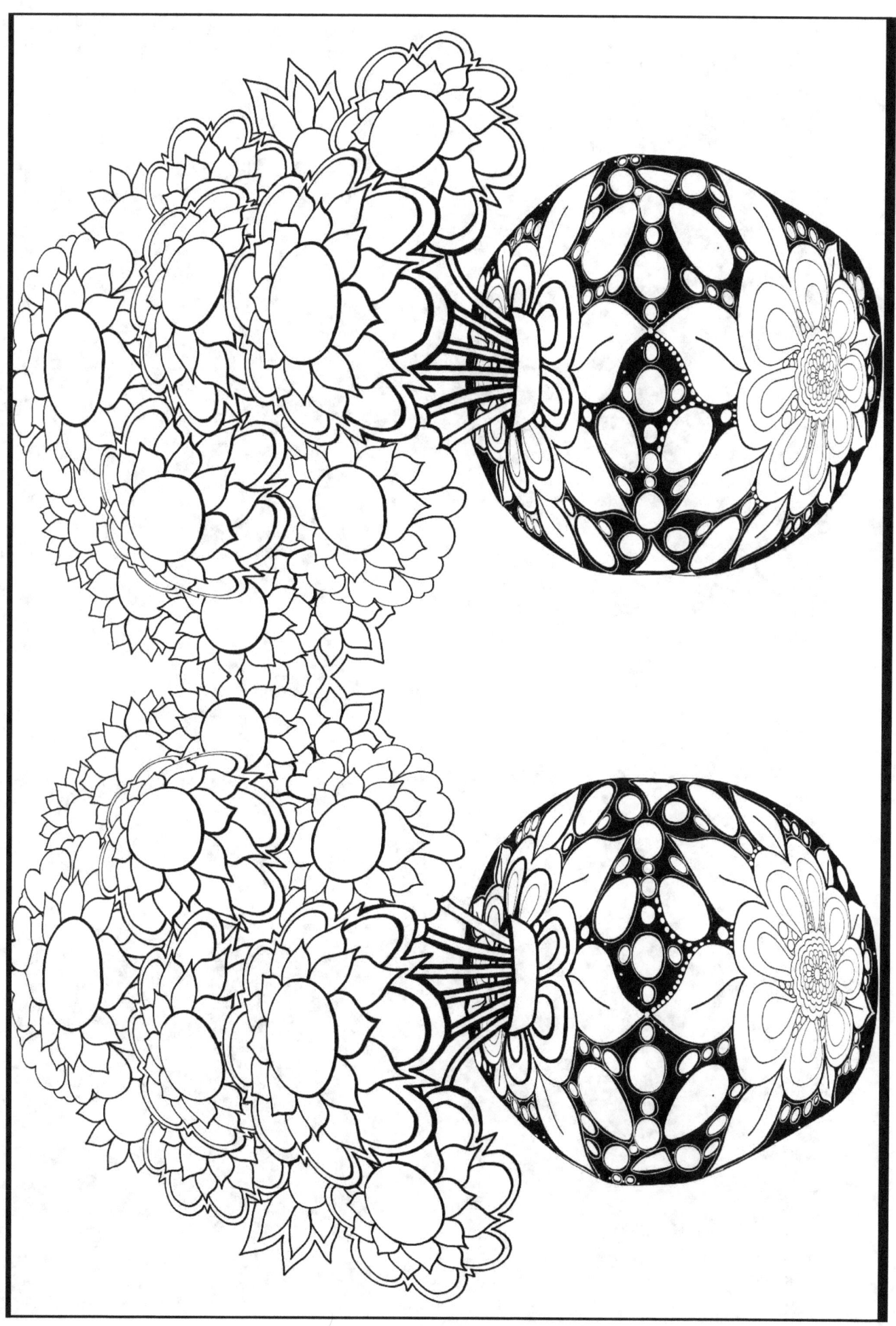

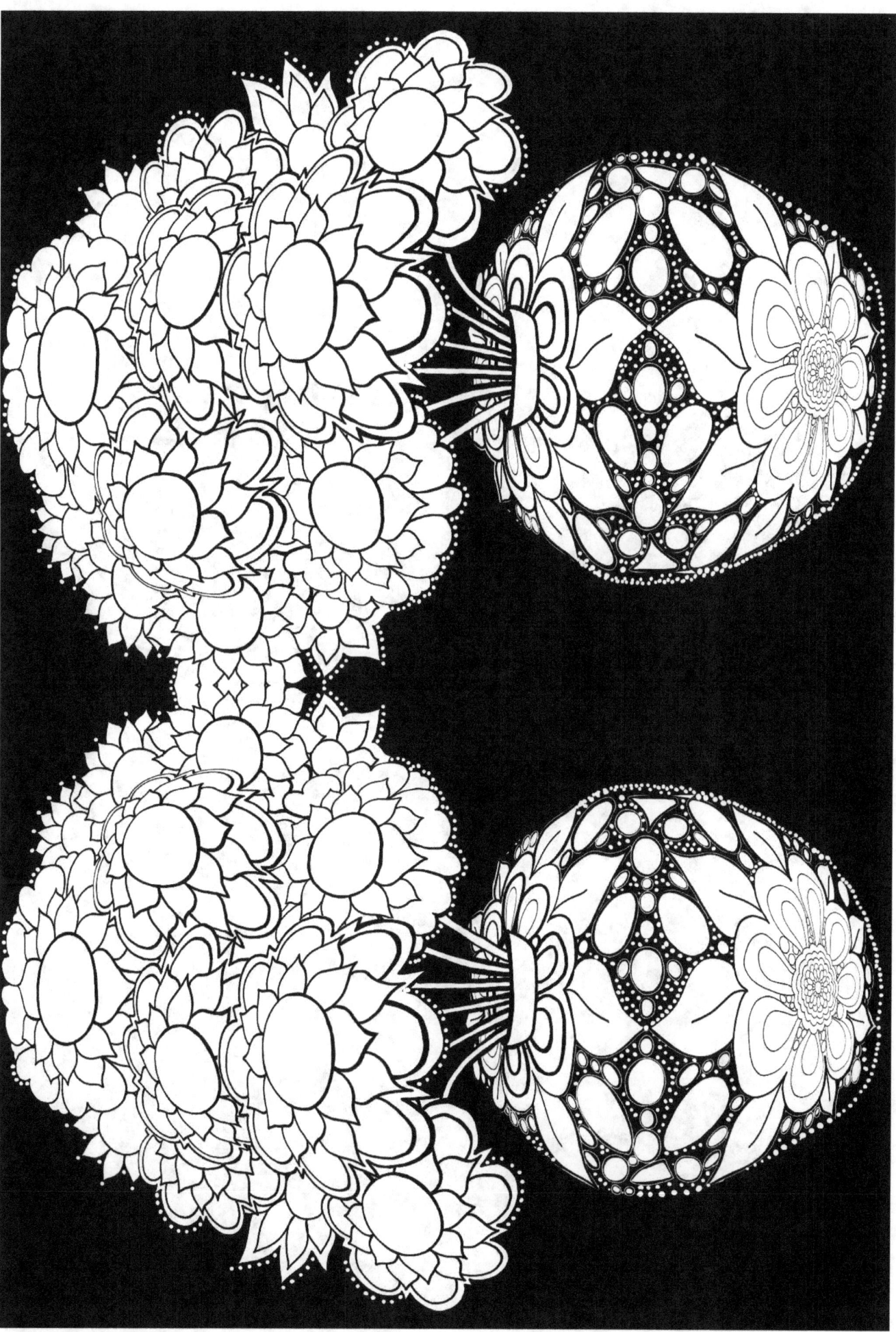

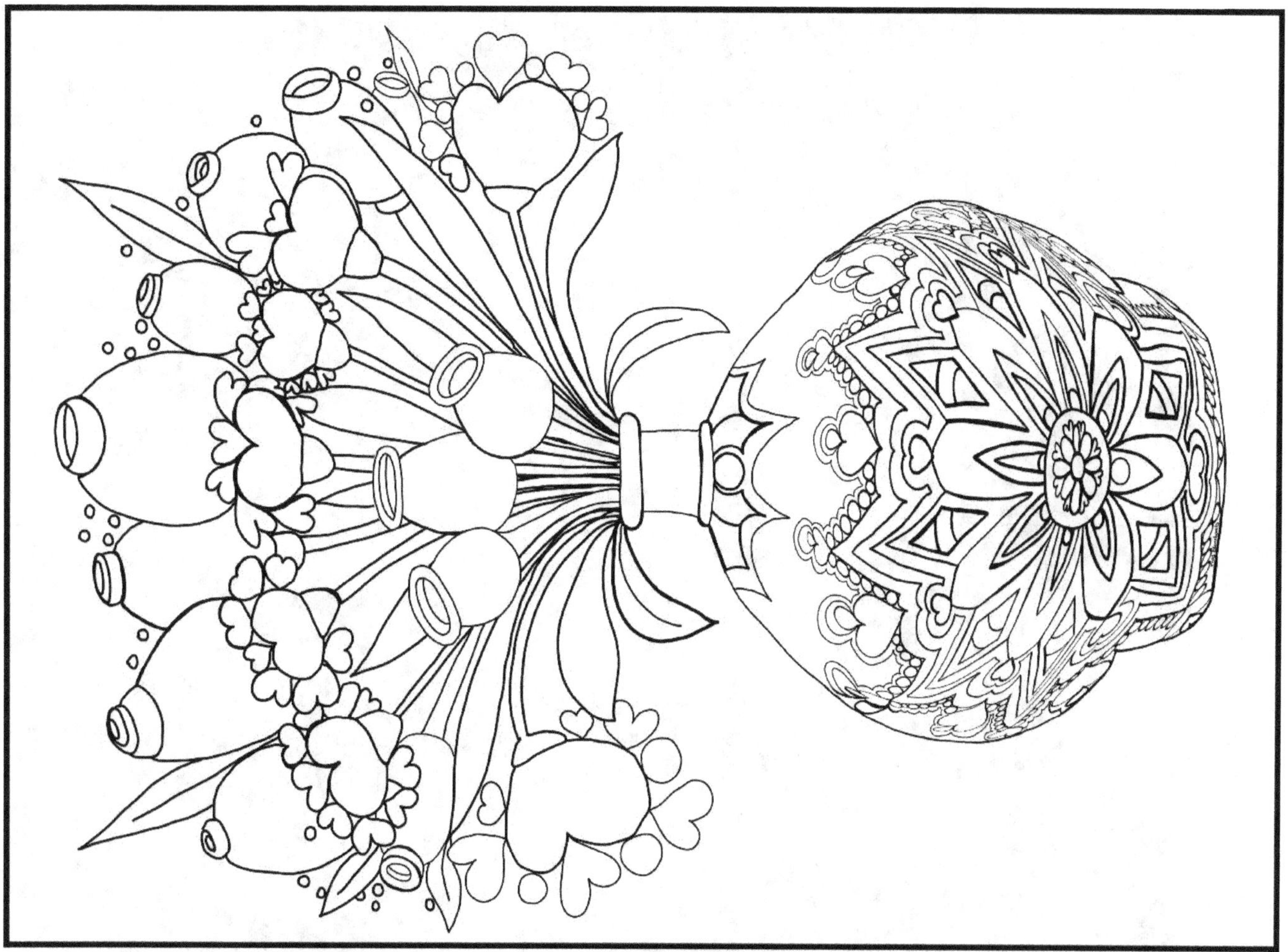

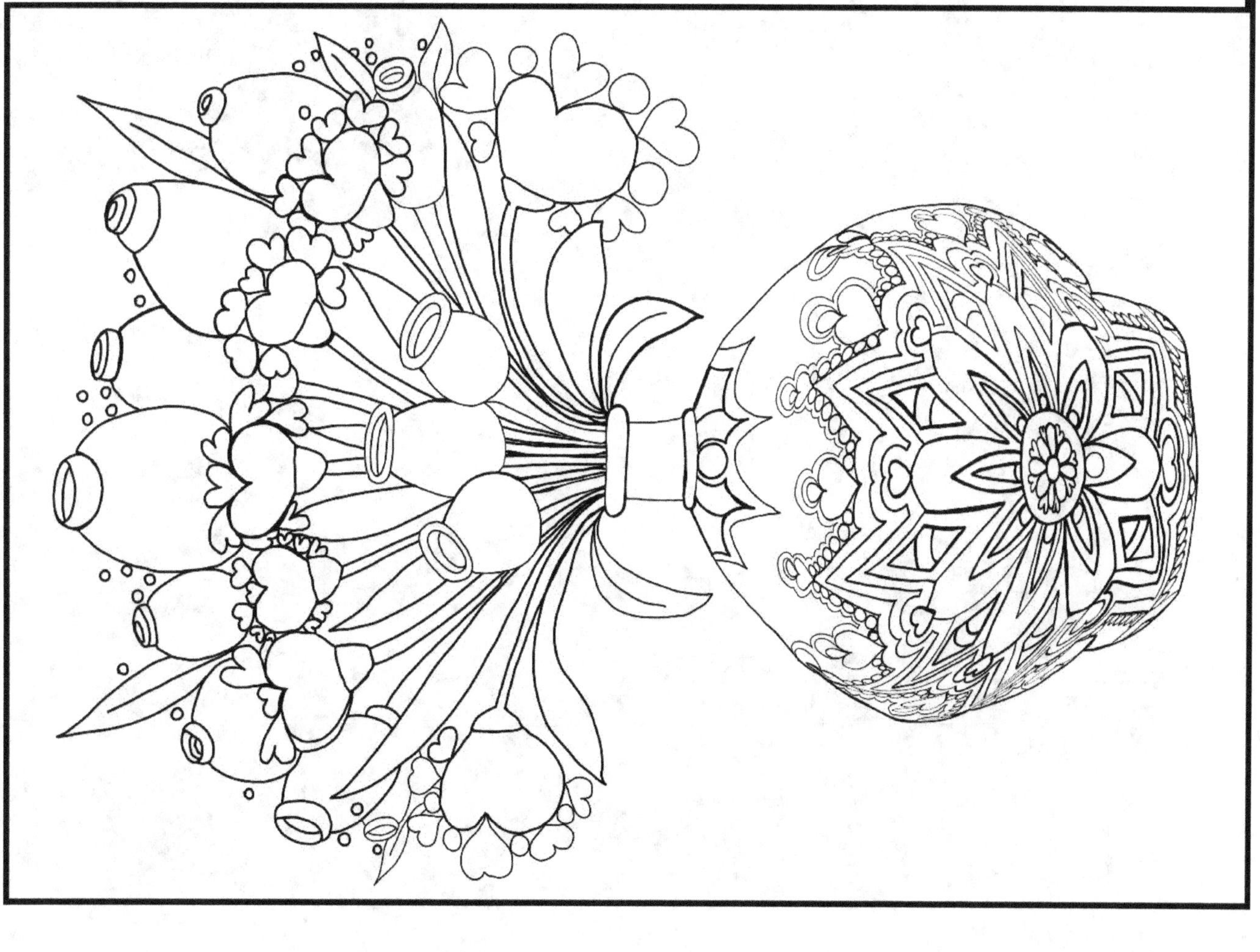

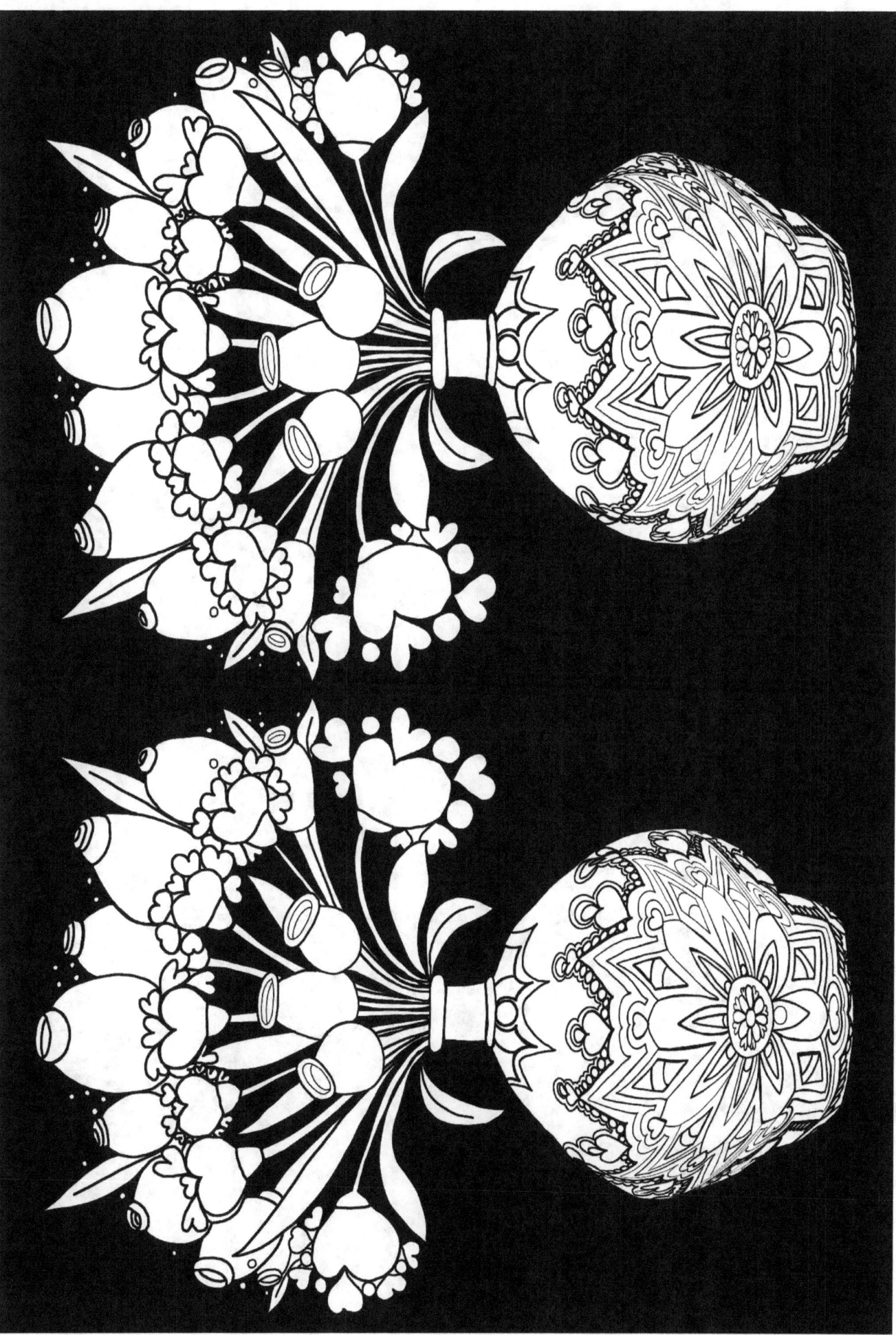

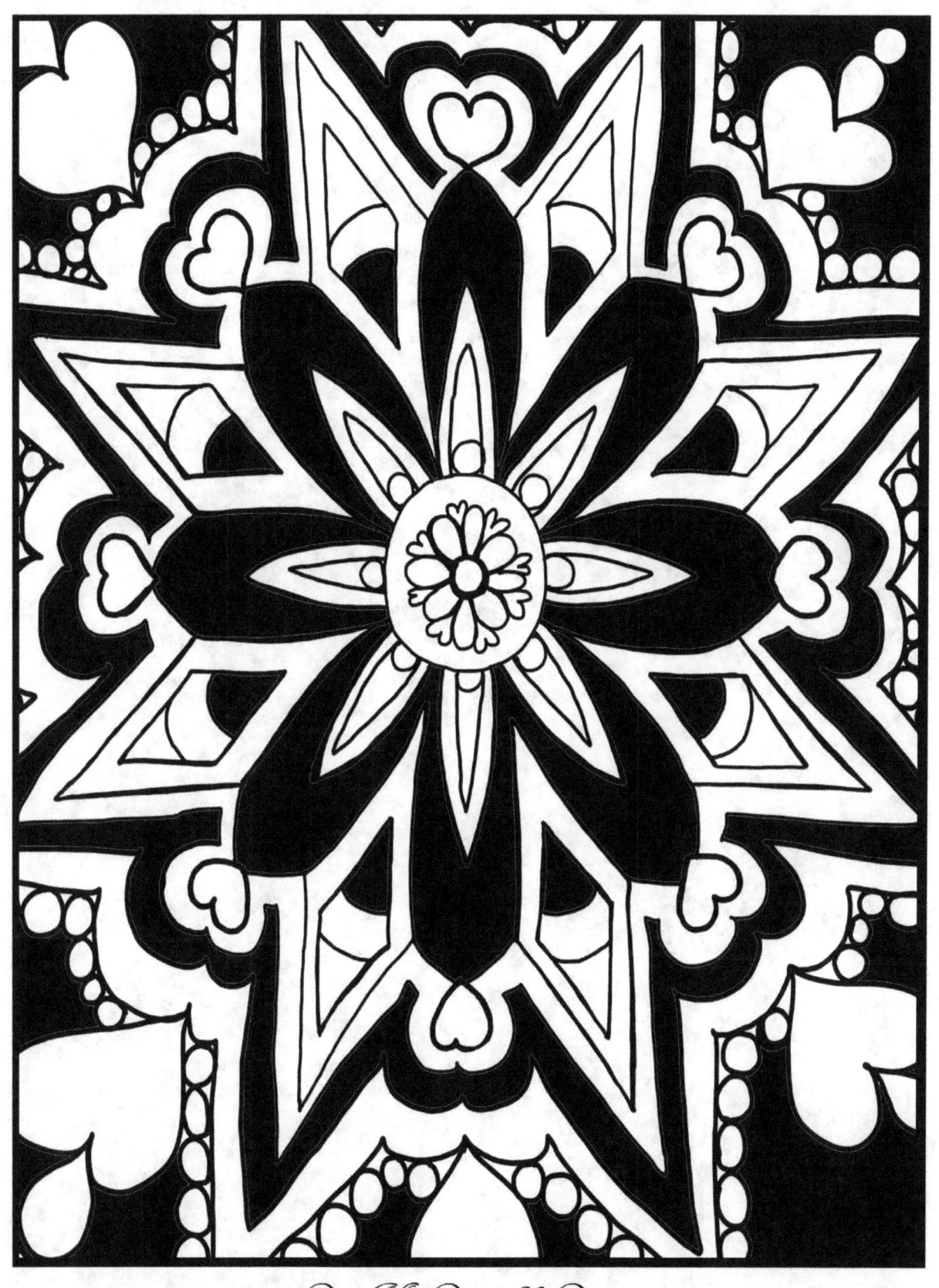

D. McDonald Designs

Extreme Mandala Coloring Book Three

D. McDonald Designs

Extreme Mandala Coloring Book Three

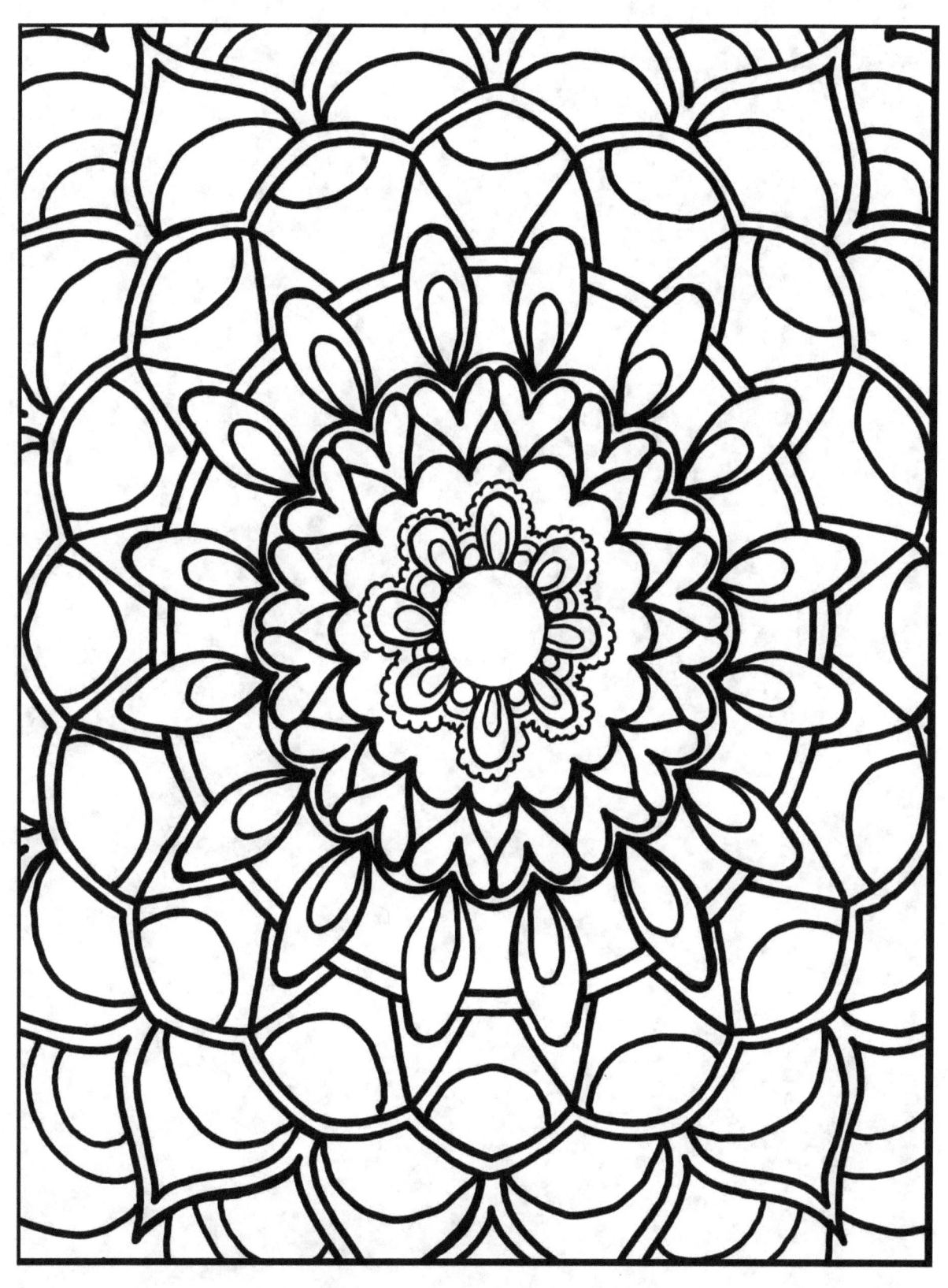

D. McDonald Designs

Extreme Mandala Coloring Book Three

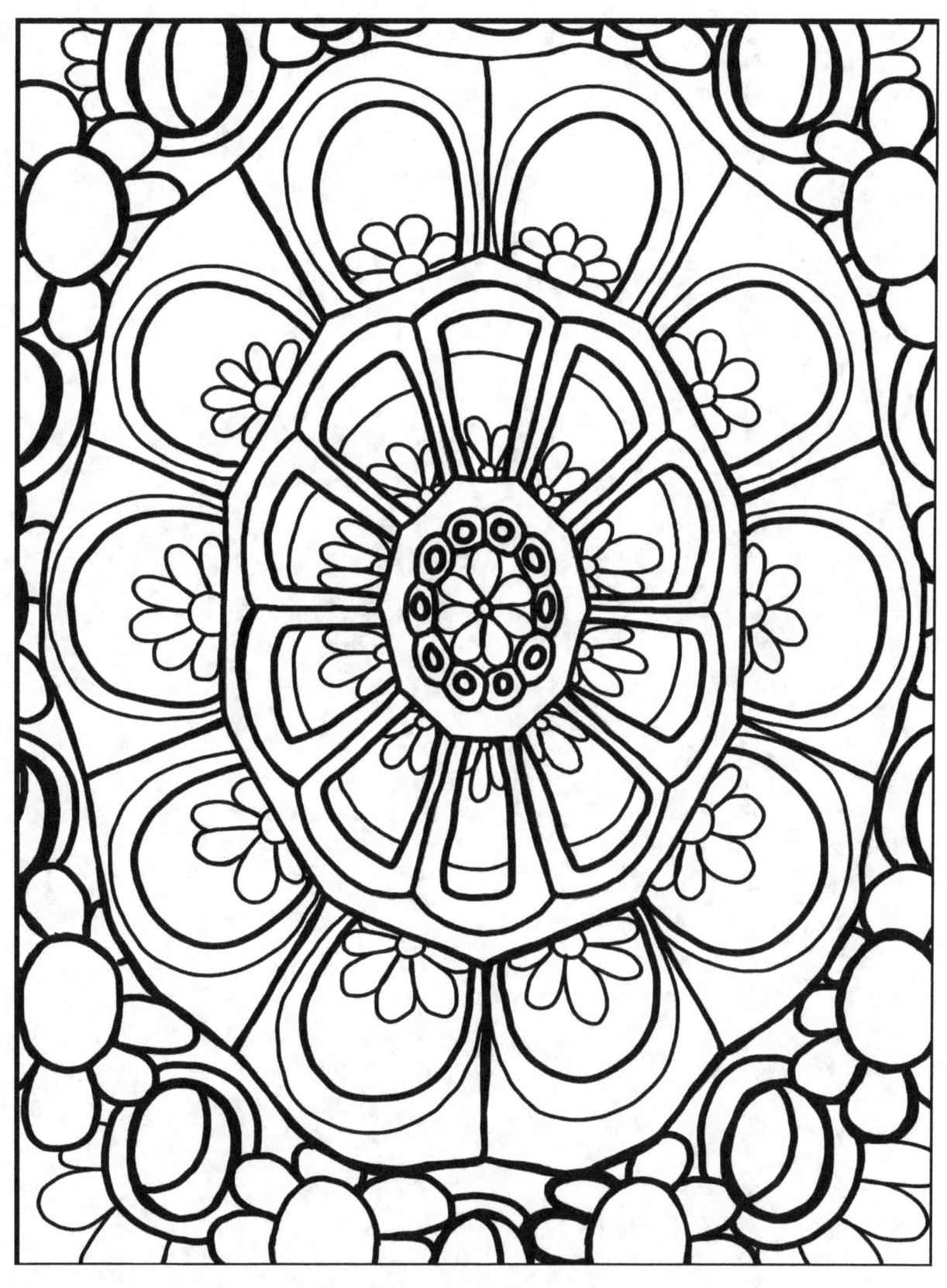

D. McDonald Designs

Extreme Mandala Coloring Book Three

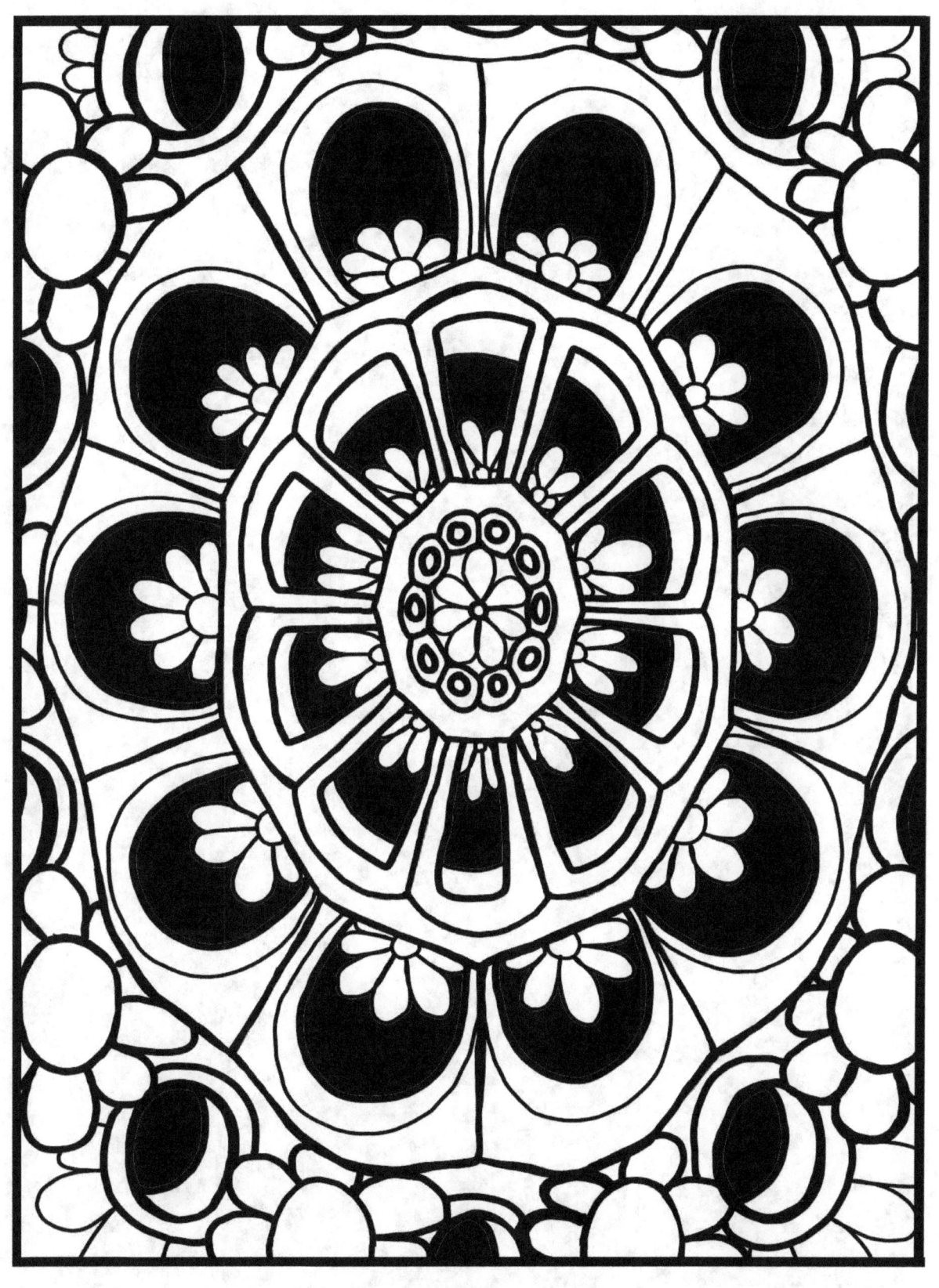

D. McDonald Designs

Extreme Mandala Coloring Book Three

D. McDonald Designs

Extreme Mandala Coloring Book Three

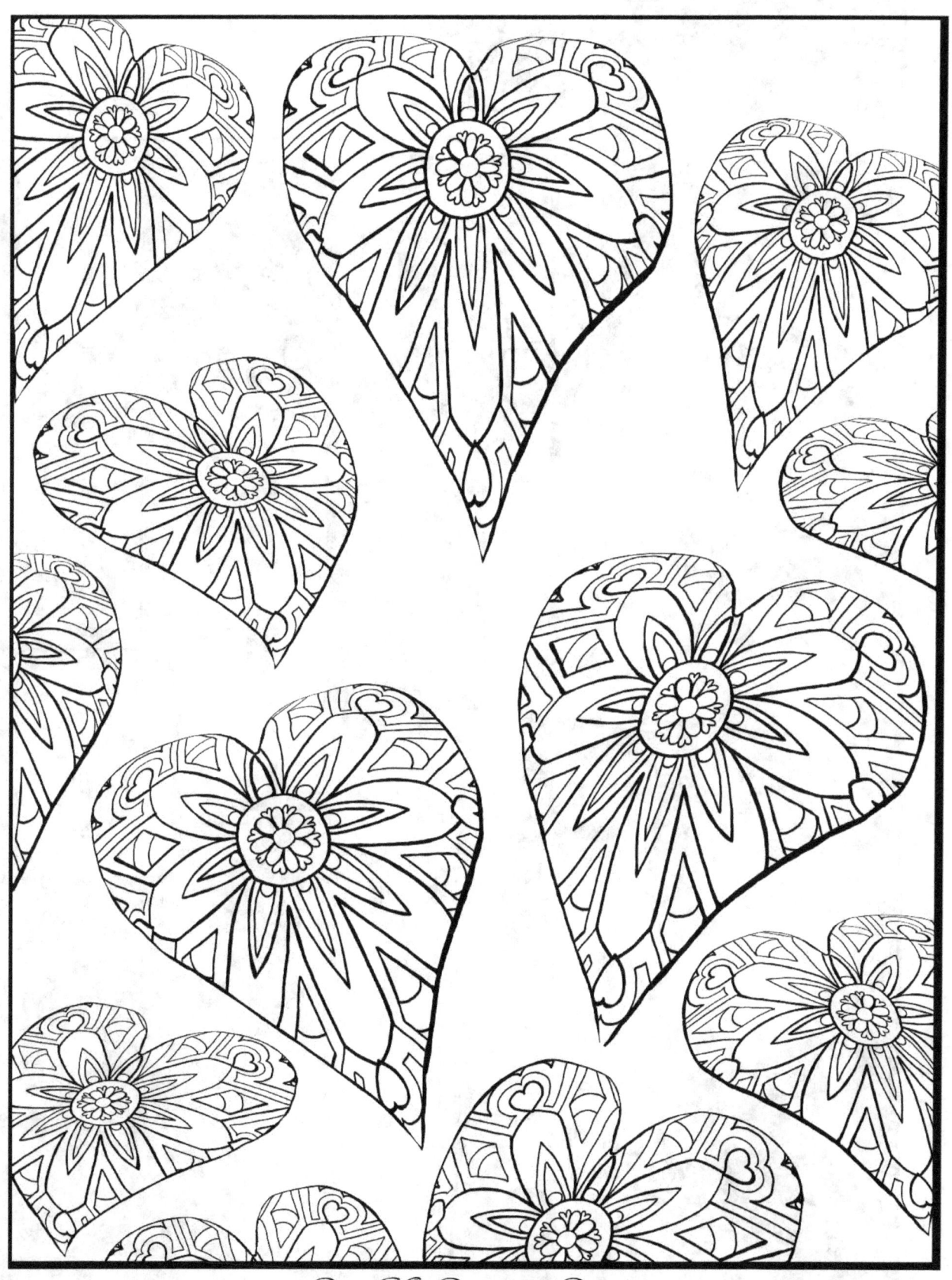

D. McDonald Designs

Extreme Mandala Hearts

Coloring Book

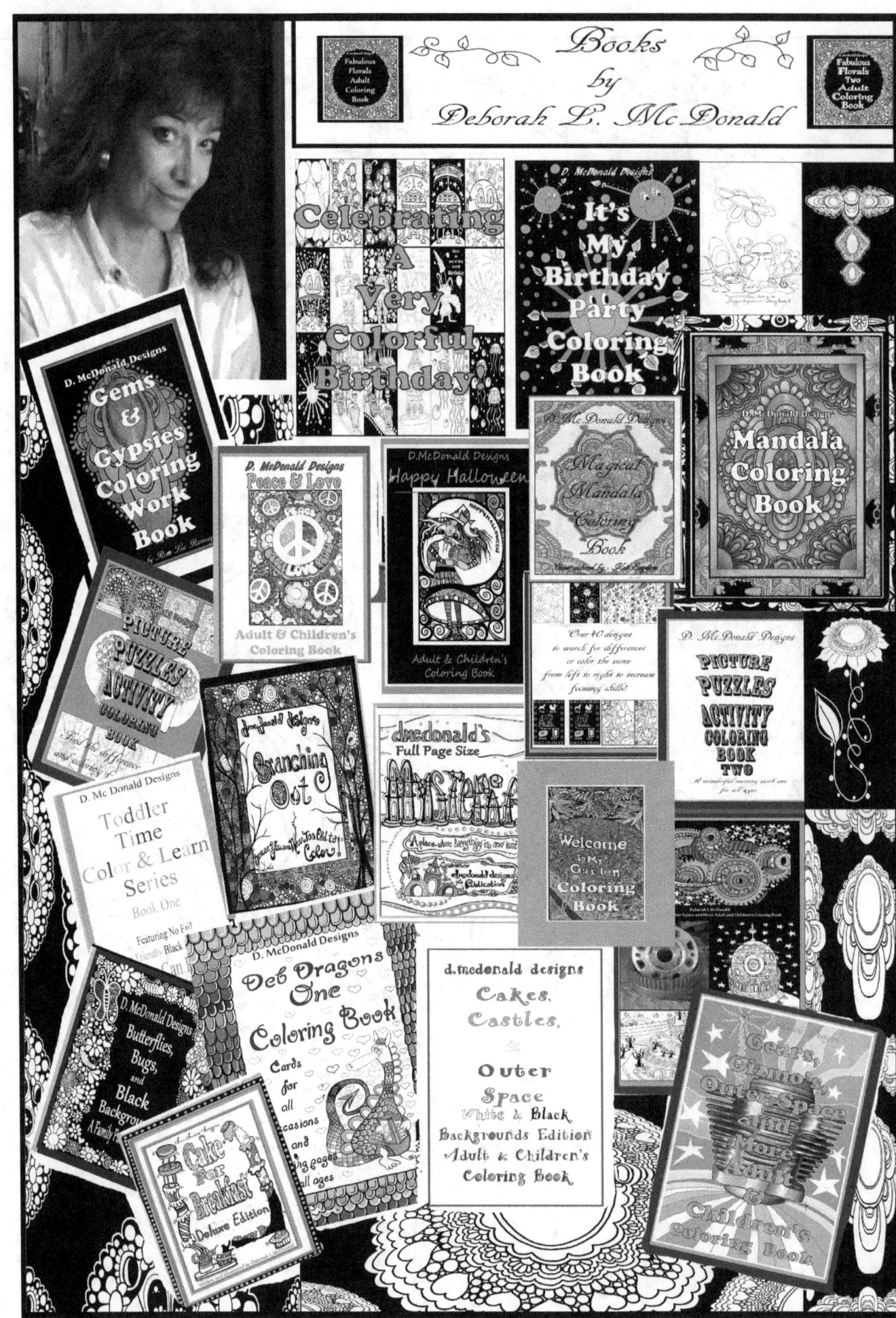

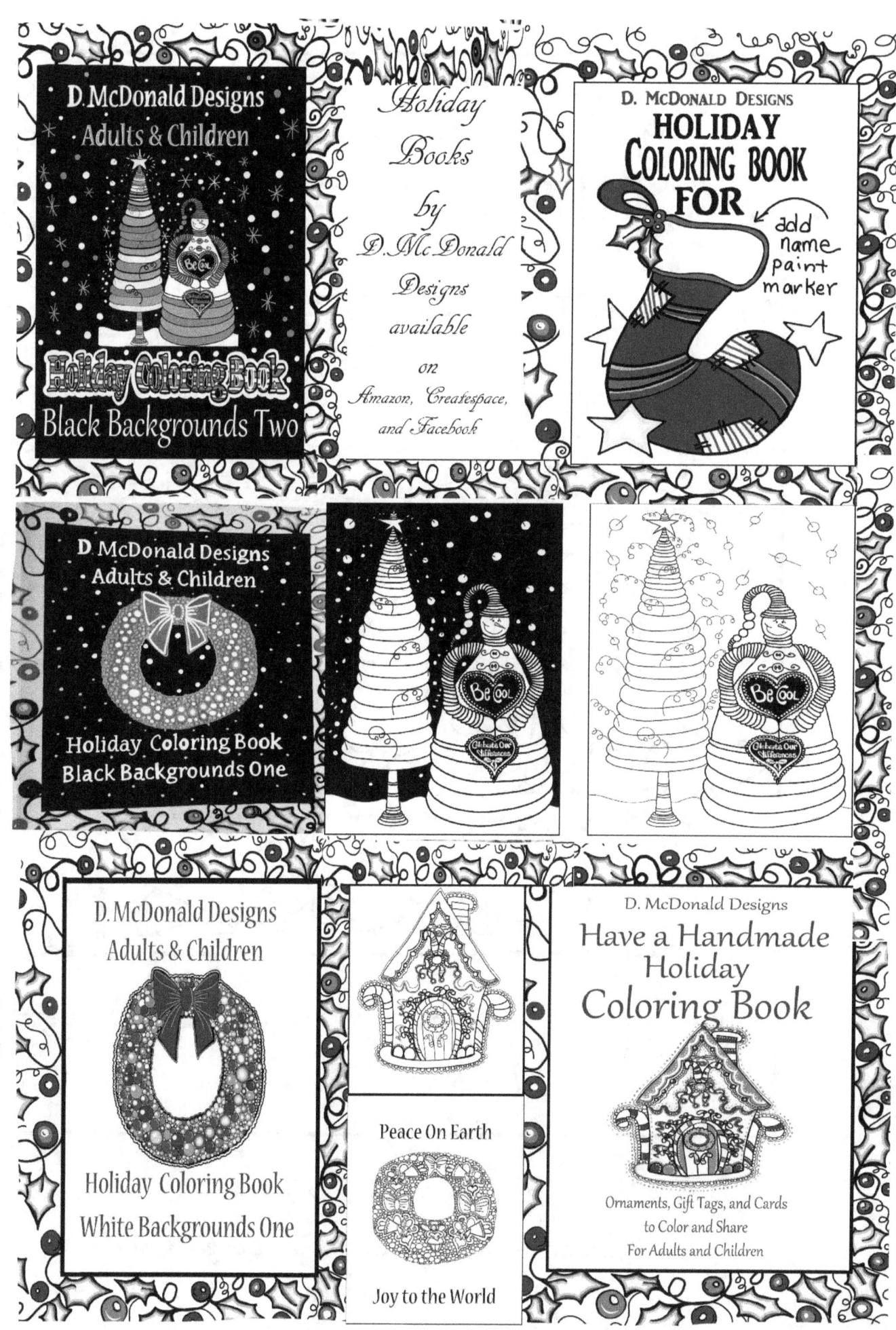

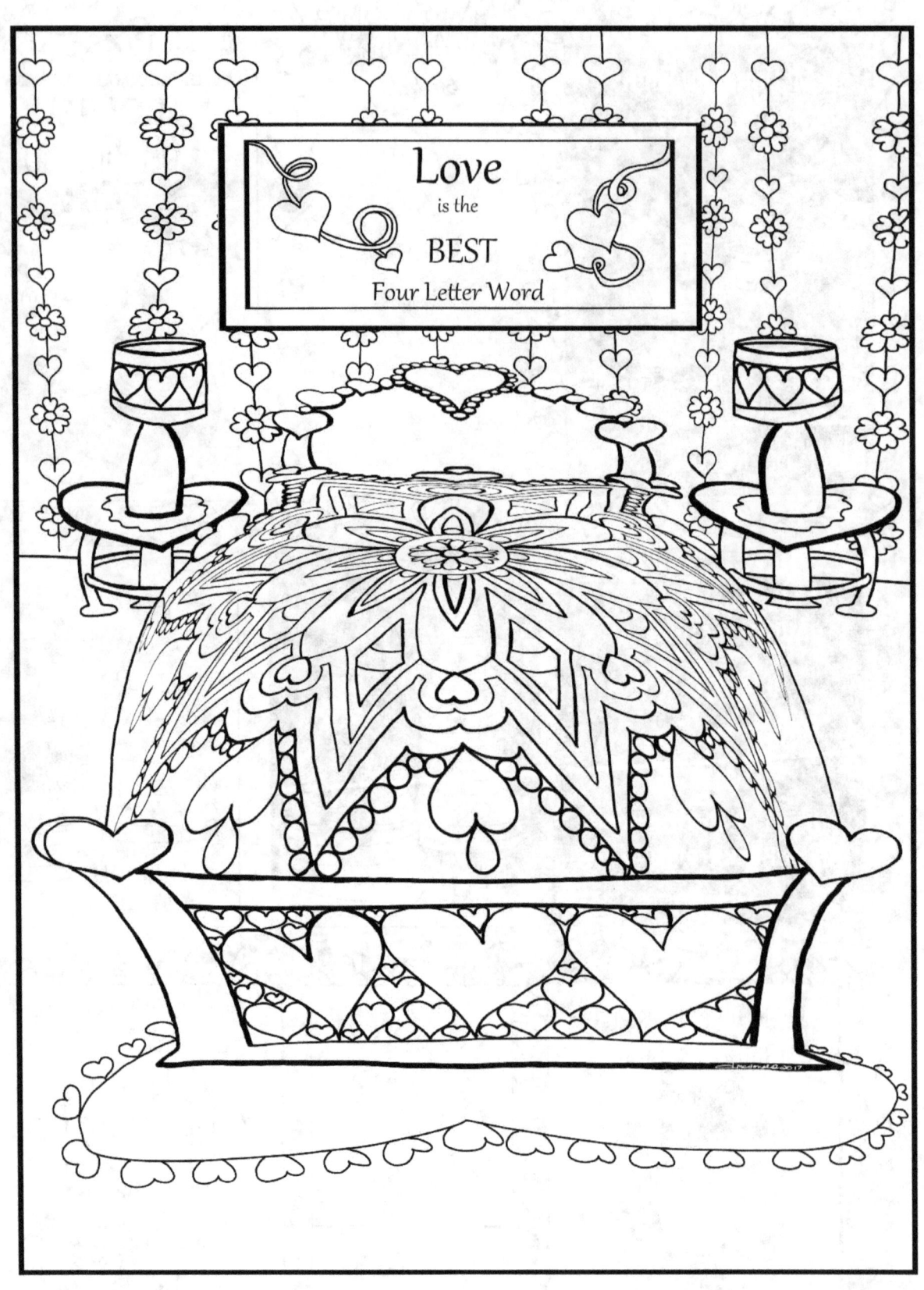

Love
is the
BEST
Four Letter Word

D. McDonald Designs
Extreme Mandala Coloring Book Two
August 2017

www.ingramcontent.com/pod-product-compliance
Lightning Source LLC
Chambersburg PA
CBHW081723220526

45468CB00008B/1952